Rapture Happened, Left Behind, What's Next!

Tribulation Period Survival Guide

By Terry J. Malone

Special thanks to Kathy Anderson and Lorayna Minear who helped edit this work.

"Rapture Happened, Left Behind, What's Next! Tribulation Survival Guide," by Terry J. Malone. ISBN: 978-1-62137-430-5 (softcover).

Published 2013 by Virtualbookworm.com Publishing Inc., P.O. Box 9949, College Station, TX, 77842, US.

Contents

Introduction

The Bible says there will come a time when the Lord will come and take His earthly Saints (Christians) out of this world in a supernatural event called the rapture of the church (I Thessalonians 4:13-18; I Corinthians 15:50-54). People from all over the world will be here one day, and suddenly, without warning, be caught up in a miraculous global disappearance.

You may be reading this book because you want to learn more about the rapture and what will follow. Or you may be one of the billions of people for which this book was created who have been left behind to face the most horrific time period in human history known as the tribulation period. If you fall into either category and do not know the Lord Jesus as Savior keep reading.

You may be wondering what's next! Has the Biblical rapture really taken place and am I really about to enter the tribulation period? Someday soon (if not already), you may be contemplating these very words. Do you know what will come next? Have you prepared a detailed plan (based on the Bible) that will maximize your chances of surviving the coming tribulation period? If you're like most, you haven't put a seconds thought into it.

That's why I wrote *RAPTURE HAPPENED, LEFT BEHIND, WHAT'S NEXT!* This book was created to provide a survival guide through the tribulation period for those left behind. This isn't just your typical survival guide; it's a survival guide based on Biblical tribulation period events. I hope to give direction as to what might happen following the rapture, the order in which events may come, and an approximate timeline as to when each event may take place. This Bible based guide gives you timely advice straight from Jesus Himself regarding this time of trouble.

I have also provided a commonsense survival section specifically designed around the events of the tribulation period. You will find that just building a basement shelter, storing food and water, and bunkering down for 7 years will not be a feasible survival strategy for this time period. When the Antichrist takes over, the world will have gone through at least one world war of epic proportions. The destruction and devastation will be so great, the Bible says, many will die out of fear (Luke 21:26) for looking upon those things that are coming on the earth. It is through this fear that the world will put their trust in the Antichrist to lead them out of certain chaos. He will immediately enforce his worldwide economic system that will require all to take his mark and worship him. Refusing to participate in his system will mean losing your job or business (income), home (whether you own or rent), freedom, and at some point, your very life.

3

You will also encounter various supernatural plagues, natural disasters and wars that will claim the lives of the majority of the global population. This will be a dangerous and perilous time whether you know (become a Christian) the Lord or not! Take a look at how the Book of Zephaniah describes this horrific time period:

> The great day of the LORD is near, it is near, and hasteth greatly, even the voice of the day of the LORD: The mighty man shall cry there bitterly. That day is a day of wrath, a day of trouble and distress, a day of wasteness and desolation, a day of darkness and gloominess, a day of clouds and thick darkness, a day of the trumpet and alarm against the fenced cities, and against the high towers. And I will bring distress upon men, that they shall walk like blind men, because they have sinned against the LORD: And their blood shall be poured out as dust, and their flesh as the dung. Neither their silver nor their gold shall be able to deliver them in the day of the LORD's wrath; but the whole land shall be devoured by the fire of his jealousy: For he shall make even a speedy riddance of all them that dwell in the land (Zephaniah 1:14-18).

This passage outlines a very gloomy and dark time filled with distress, perplexity, and complete and utter desolation worldwide. Without careful preparation that is tailored to the events of the tribulation period you will have little chance of surviving.

With that said, although surviving the tribulation period will be extremely difficult (Matthew 24:21), it's not impossible. This book is designed to make you aware of the events to come in order, providing tips, safeguards, and timely advice that could ultimately save your life.

I trust the information found in this book will provide solid survival guidance (from a Biblical perspective) through this most horrible time period.

May the Lord protect you and keep you safe.

Part 1:
Things You Need To Know & Survival Tips

As In The Days Of Noah

Just as in Noah's day, men were eating and drinking, and living out their lives to the fullest. Many scoffed at the announcement of God's imminent judgment. But just as He said, the rains came and shocked the world.

One day, very soon, Jesus will come and rapture the church. There won't be any fanfare or warning, and He'll only take those who are truly His. In a moment, in the twinkling of an eye, you and your surroundings (Christians) will change forever (I Corinthians 15:50-52). For those who are left behind, they will suffer through the most horrible time in the history of mankind known as the tribulation period. This period will last 7 years.

Just over six thousand years ago, the age of man began with the six days of creation and the origination of man. Because of the sin of man, fellowship with God was broken. To restore fellowship, God sent His Son to die, bearing our sins on the cross, and rise again three days later. When He left, He said He would come again and take away those who are His own.

Here we are, almost two thousand years later, still awaiting the return of the Lord. "...Where is the promise of his coming? For since the fathers fell asleep, all things continue as they were from the beginning of the creation (II Peter 3:4)." Every generation has proclaimed this statement since

8

our Lord made this promise. Unfortunately, because of the lack of Biblical knowledge, many, including Christians, will be caught unaware when He does come. If only they would have been able to discern the time that they were living in. As Jesus stated of the Pharisees, they were able to perceive the weather, but unable to discern the coming of the Son of Man (Matthew 16:3).

You may say, "What's different about this generation that sets it apart from the previous?" Plenty, but there is one very significant event that makes this generation unique, the rebirth of Israel. Jesus said that in the generation in which Israel again becomes a nation, a generation would not pass until He returns (Matthew 24:34). That prediction did not come true until this generation. Since the early days of the Roman Empire, Jews have been scattered throughout the world. However, on May 14, 1948, in one day, that all changed and Israel was reborn as a nation just as the Bible predicted (Isaiah 66:7-8)!

Jesus is coming again and will shock the world, just as He did in the days of Noah. Only one generation saw that happen and only one will witness His return.

What Is The Rapture Of The Church?

The rapture of the church, described mainly in I Corinthians 15:50-55 and I Thessalonians 4:13-18, states there will come a time when the

Lord will descend from heaven and remove all Christians from the earth in the moment in the twinkling of an eye. From that day forward Christians will forever be with the Lord. "Rapture" comes from the words "caught up". In the Greek the word is "harpazo" means to "seize upon by force" or "to snatch up".

The Bible says this snatching up or catching away could take place at any moment, but it will only happen to those who know the Lord as Savior.

At this point in time, it is believed that once the rapture takes place, God will pour out His wrath upon mankind in a time period called the seven-year tribulation period. The Bible says this seven- year period will be the most horrible time in history (Luke 21:25-26).

Who Will Be Taken?

> And Enoch lived sixty and five years, and begat Methuselah: And Enoch walked with God after he begat Methuselah three hundred years, and begat sons and daughters: And all the days of Enoch were three hundred sixty and five years: And Enoch walked with God: and he was not; for God took him (Genesis 5:21-24).

In the Book of Genesis, we find a man named
Enoch, of the line of Seth, that the Bible
specifically points out as being a man that
walked with God. But there's more! He was
also taken by God. Many Bible scholars have
attributed this mysterious disappearance
(taking) as a picture of the future rapture of
the church. Later, in the Book of Jude, this
same Enoch would give us a glimpse of what
will take place at the second coming of Christ:

> And Enoch also, the seventh from
> Adam, prophesied of these, saying,
> Behold, the Lord cometh with ten
> thousands of his saints, to execute
> judgment upon all, and to convince
> all that are ungodly among them of
> all their ungodly deeds which they
> have ungodly committed, and of all
> their hard speeches which ungodly
> sinners have spoken against him.
> These are murmurers, complainers,
> walking after their own lusts; and
> their mouth speaketh great swelling
> words, having men's persons in
> admiration because of advantage.
> But, beloved, remember ye the
> words which were spoken before of
> the apostles of our Lord Jesus
> Christ; How that they told you there
> should be mockers in the last time,
> who should walk after their own
> ungodly lusts. These be they who

separate themselves, sensual, having not the Spirit (Jude 14-19).

In Genesis 5:24, an important characteristic of Enoch's relationship with God is emphasized in that "Enoch walked with God". If this is indeed a picture of the rapture, and I believe it is, is it possible that the same criteria to be taken in the future rapture will be determined by whether or not we are walking with God? This is a sobering thought in light of today's liberal so-called Christian churches. I'm afraid many church members are going to be shocked when they find themselves left behind to go through the most horrible time in world history.

Neighbor, it's time to determine if you are truly walking with God! Certainly, the Lord is at hand and if you expect to go with Him when He raptures the church, you will have to be walking with Him. And you'll have to be ready before He comes or you won't go!

You may say, what is the criterion for going? I'm glad you asked that question...here it is. You're going to have to have a personal relationship (walk) with the Lord just as Enoch did if you expect to be taken during the rapture. That relationship has been given various names over the years, but the truth is, if you don't have Jesus as Lord of your life you will not go when the trumpet blasts. On that day, it won't matter what religious affiliation you may have, only those who hear His voice will go. Today is the day to examine your heart and determine if you truly are living for the Lord.

You may say, "I'm not sure if I would go if the trumpet sounded...but I'd like to settle that today." Well, you can solve that problem right now by praying this simple prayer, repenting of your sins, and turning your life over to the Lord from this day forward. If you would like to accept Jesus as Lord, please pray with me right now:

Father, I know that I am a sinner and cannot obtain salvation in and of myself. I come to You in the name of Jesus asking that You forgive me of my sins, and to cleanse me from all unrighteousness and guilt. I trust and believe that Jesus died and rose again to pay my sin penalty. I accept this free gift of salvation, and from this day forward, turn my life completely over to the Lord. I thank You and praise You God for giving me a new life in Christ. Amen.

If you prayed this prayer and meant every word you are now a Christian and on your way to heaven.

From this day forward, life will never be the same. It is likely you may have to die for your belief in Christ. Stand strong and be of good courage and the Lord will strengthen and guide you to come out victorious even in the face of death.

Commit your life to Jesus today before it's too late!

Tribulation Period Begins & Significant Signs You Should Be Aware Of

I guess the obvious question is what's next! Once the rapture takes place, the next step will be the start of the seven-year tribulation period, but that might not begin right away. It could be days, weeks, months or even years before the tribulation period begins. But when it does, it will last 7 years (360 days x 7 years) or 2,520 days (1,260 days per half of tribulation period; Revelation 11:2-3). This is a precise timeline and will not last one day longer than the Bible has prophesied.

You should be aware of some of the signs that will mark the significant milestones of the tribulation period. One, you will know day one when the tribulation period begins when a man rises up and confirms a seven-year peace accord with Israel (Daniel 9:27). Most Bible scholars believe he will rise up out of the European Union. When this event takes place, you know day one of the tribulation period has begun.

At the same time the Antichrist confirms a peace accord with Israel, two of God's supernatural witnesses will begin preaching the Gospel on the streets of Jerusalem. These two men will openly preach the Gospel and will be openly hated for doing so. They will be so hated many will attempt to kill them, but God will empower them with supernatural power and will not allow them to be harmed. In fact, by whatever means a person may try to kill them, that person will immediately die that death (Revelation 11:5). They will also have power over weather to stop the rain from falling, to perform miraculous plagues whenever and on whomsoever they wish, and to turn any body of water into blood (Revelation 11:6). Most Bible prophecy experts believe they will stop the rain from falling worldwide for the first 3½ years of the tribulation period.

They will be unstoppable in their mission to spread the Gospel. Their ministry will be confined to Jerusalem, however, they will be well known worldwide. They will be dressed in sackcloth and will have the power to call down fire from heaven or smite the world with various plagues whenever they choose (Revelation 11:6). Even the Antichrist will be powerless to destroy them during the first 3½ years (Revelation 11:7-8). They will perform great miracles and induce a worldwide revival that will be simply mind-boggling and undeniable.

At the midway point of the tribulation period (1,260 days), the two witnesses will be killed. Shortly after their death, they will come back to life and slowly be raptured to heaven for all the world to see (Revelation 11:10-13).

On day 1,261, the Antichrist will desecrate the Jerusalem Temple, declare himself to be God, and demand worship. His assistant, the false prophet, will erect a statue and cause it to speak. He will introduce a new world system that will require everyone to take an identification mark (666) in order to buy or sell (Revelation 13:11-18).

This event will most likely mean the end of land or home ownership for anyone who does not take his mark. I suspect all utilities such as water, sewage, electricity, and heat will immediately be discontinued for anyone not registered with the newly created world system. Depending how quickly the world conforms to the system of the Antichrist, you can expect eviction from your home to follow. Frankly, I wouldn't expect a peaceful eviction either. Soon, you and your family will be fugitives on the run with no more than the clothes on their back and what little they can carry. How you have planned in advance for this day could mean the difference between life and death.

On day 2,520 the tribulation period will end and the second coming of Christ will take place the next day.

To summarize, when you see the Middle East peace agreement confirmed and the appearance of these two witnesses know that you are living in the beginning of the tribulation period. The Battle of Gog and Magog (Ezekiel 38 & 39) will likely come in the early stages of the tribulation period (likely within the first year) followed by the rebuilding of the Holy Temple (Revelation 11:1-2) and the revealing of the Ark of the Covenant.

On my website, Calvary Prophecy Report, you will find a short video that will give you a likely scenario of what could happen following the Antichrist's confirmation of the peace agreement titled *12 Events That Will Immediately Take Place Following The Rapture.* Do an internet search on that title and watch the video.

Surviving The Tribulation Period

If you're reading this survival guide, it may be because you didn't get taken in the rapture of the church, but you can still know Jesus as Lord and Savior. I hope this will be a tool that the Lord uses to open up your eyes to your need for Him. Your future and eternity could depend on what you decide at this very moment. Don't let this opportunity to know the Lord pass you by. It may be your last!

The next question that will likely come to mind, will you be able to survive what the Bible says will be the most horrible time in history? I have always questioned if there are specific procedures that one could follow that would enable a person to survive the tribulation period. I truly believe that it will be by the grace of God that anyone survives. Let me put this time period in perspective. The tribulation period will be so devastating and so horrible that Jesus said, "And except those days should be shortened, there should no flesh be saved: But for the elect's sake those days shall be shortened (Matthew 24:22)." However, the Bible is clear that there will be survivors, and it could be you!

So what are your chances of surviving the tribulation period? Nobody knows for sure, but we do know that one-quarter of the world's population will be eliminated (Revelation 6:7-8) when the fourth seal is broken and another one-third will die when the sixth trumpet sounds (Revelation 9:13-19). That doesn't even include:

1. The complete destruction of Mystery Babylon (Revelation 18).
2. The devastation of a worldwide earthquake (Revelation 16:18).
3. The complete annihilation of the Russian-Islamic Alliance (Ezekiel 38 and 39).
4. Wormwood (Revelation 8:10 -11).
5. The Battle of Armageddon (Revelation 9:16; 16:15-16).
6. The worldwide martyrdom of Christians (Revelation 7:13-17).
7. The worldwide hailstorm of 100 lb. hailstones (Revelation 16:21).
8. The earth being struck by a giant meteorite (Revelation 8:8-9).

Certainly, this is not a complete list but you get the picture. If there are survivors, a person's chances of being in that number are slim. But by the grace of God, I believe this book can increase your chances significantly.

How To Survive The Tribulation Period With Survival Tips From a Biblical Perspective

It is unlikely that the following information regarding surviving the tribulation period will be of any value to anyone prior to the rapture of the church. This information is intended for those who have found themselves on the other side of the rapture (left behind) awaiting the beginning of the tribulation period.

The purpose of this section is to determine the best survival techniques, based on the Bible, for surviving the tribulation period. Frankly, it will be difficult for anyone accurately to plan for the horrible events of the tribulation period, because it's more than just anarchy and war. There will be many supernatural catastrophes sent by God that are designed to systematically destroy every resource man must have to survive. They will be specific and many times only target certain natural resources while completely disregarding others. Here are some of those precise events that will take place during this time:

1. First trumpet: All grass burnt up; one-third of trees burnt up (Revelation 8:7).

2. Third trumpet: One-third of world's rivers and streams poisoned (Revelation 8:10-11).
3. First bowl: Sores breakout only on those who have taken the mark (Revelation 16:2)
4. Second bowl: Sea turns to blood, all fish die (Revelation 16:3).
5. Third bowl: Rivers and fountains become blood (Revelation 16:4).
6. Fourth bowl: Heat of the sun scorches men (Revelation 16:8-9).
7. Fifth bowl: Complete darkness falls only on the kingdom of the Antichrist (Revelation 16:10).

By the first trumpet judgment, much of what acts as a continuous natural filter to clean our air will be destroyed. The first bowl judgment will see sores breakout only on those who have taken the mark of the Antichrist. The third trumpet, and second and third bowl judgments, will see virtually all water sources polluted or destroyed. God will systematically bring man to what looks to be the end of the world and many times only on specific targets.

Couple these supernatural and systematic plagues with the above listed wars, and there looks to be little hope of survival even if one does plan ahead. This book is designed to take what the Bible says and use its information to dramatically increase your chances.

The following will give you an advance look at what some of the obstacles may be according to the Bible, how you might be able to overcome them, and options that are just out of the question. Let's take a look at some of the general preparations and obstacles that one will likely face during this time period.

First, you wouldn't necessarily need to begin your site preparation (shelter) until you are sure the tribulation period has begun. The Bible has clear signs as to when that day will come (see *The Tribulation Period Begins*). As mentioned in an earlier section, the first sign will be when the Antichrist comes forward and confirms a peace accord with Israel and many other nations (Daniel 9:27). At around the same time, the second sign will emerge when two witnesses of God begin their supernatural ministry on the streets of Jerusalem where they will preach the gospel for 3½ years. You will certainly hear about them because they will be world-famous or infamous due to the miracles they will perform and the plagues they will send (Revelation 11:3-8). When you see these two events happening, you know the tribulation period has begun. This is the moment when I would begin my survival preparation or at least within the first year. It would be a good idea to have a thorough understanding of tribulation period events in chronological order. This is covered in detail later in this book.

Second, when the Antichrist introduces his mark, do not take it under any circumstance including threat of death (Revelation 14:9-11) to you and/or your family. Once you take the mark you are doomed eternally to death and the lake of fire.

Third, to survive the tribulation period, you have to be willing to live in places others would not even consider and terrain most would not tread. For centuries, people have lived and thrived in extreme desert places, frozen mountains, dense jungles and forests. These locations, in most cases, will require specific skills and knowledge to survive, but it can be done. At some point, you will have to leave behind the comforts of modern-day society. Your research should begin with finding such a location.

Seeking Shelter

Your first concern should be to secure a safe shelter to house you and your family, and store supplies that will sustain them for at least 3½ years of the seven-year tribulation period. Most Bible scholars believe, for the most part, the first few years won't likely be life-threatening (depending on where you live) nor will it require the mark of the Antichrist to survive. However, midway through the tribulation, the Antichrist will desecrate the Temple in Jerusalem and declare himself to be God (Daniel 9:27). From this day forward, he will push his new world economic order and require all of mankind to take his mark in order to buy or sell. When this system is instituted worldwide, without the mark, you will be unable to function in the civilized world.

But getting back to your need to secure a safe shelter location. This will likely require the purchase of land. You can either build a shelter or buy land with a shelter already pre-built. In planning your location, you should get as far away from any major city as possible. Metropolitan areas will be the first targets struck in the event of nuclear war.

Any new building structure would require permits and government permission. No matter where you go, all land and property must be registered to an owner under today's (US) system. In the new world order, I have to believe the government (Antichrist) will require everyone to reregister their land, shelter, vehicles, watercraft, planes, etc., under each person's given new mark. If you do not take the mark I can't imagine that you will be able to own property, land or transportation vehicles of any kind. So it will be difficult, if not impossible, to maintain a hidden residence where you can stockpile supplies for the last half of the tribulation period (3½ years).

Probably the best option to consider is to scout out natural shelters such as caves, rocky crevices, abandoned houses and tunnels, and large trees for a possible tree house shelter. This should be done well in advance.

A portable option to consider would be a large tent. Many of today's tents are light weight, yet durable, and can be assembled and taken down in a few easy steps. This would allow you to move quickly from location to location as the days become increasingly dangerous (see Survival Resources section; The Survival Zone).

Of course, living out in nature will have its own dangers during this time period. The Bible says, following the breaking of the fourth seal judgment (war; Revelation 6:7-8), one-quarter of the world's population will die, and one of the means by which they will die is by the beasts of the earth. Many Bible prophecy scholars interpret this to mean, during this time, God will remove the natural fear of man from wild animals. Due to the lack of available food, mankind will become one of nature's primary food sources.

Nuclear War

Another danger that will come from this great world war is the effect of radioactive fallout on nature. With so many people dying in so little time, one has to believe that nuclear weapons will be the weapon of choice. This will greatly affect your ability to live off the land, plant crops, or drink water from available natural sources. However, it is simply unknown what the full extent of damage these wars will cause on the earth during this time. Location selection will be important to avoid nuclear fallout. Stay far away from metro areas that are likely to be nuclear targets.

In general, you can use any plant food that is ready for harvest if you can effectively decontaminate it (peel skin or scrub with water). Growing plants, however, can absorb some radioactive materials through their leaves as well as from the soil, especially if rains have occurred during or after the fallout period. Avoid using these plants for food except in an emergency. As always, it is best to boil all water (you'll need a pot, plastic bottle or tinfoil) for at least five minutes to kill all contaminants. However, boiling water will not remove radioactive fallout or particles. We will discuss that in more detail later.

Supplies

Now let's get to the supplies you will need in order to survive through the 3½ year reign of the Antichrist. Remember, you can't buy, sell or hold a job for at least 3½ years without the mark. All food and supplies will have to be paid for, transported, and stored in a safe place before this new system is put in place. Of course, it will probably take some time (weeks maybe months) before the mark is properly instituted and enforced worldwide, but if you wait until the revealing of the Antichrist you may run into a critical food and supply shortage. If you remember, once the Antichrist declares himself to be God and introduces the mark (Revelation 13:11-18), God will send out angels to warn the world not to take the mark of beast (Revelation 14:6-7, 9-11). I have to believe anyone who orders or attempts to purchase large quantities of food and supplies beyond this moment will be viewed with great suspicion by the government. Even if you are permitted to purchase the needed supplies, you will most definitely run into severe shortages. Your wisest move is to plan ahead, make a list, and spread your purchases out over the early part of the first 3½ years of the tribulation period. There's no guarantee when the world war described in Revelation chapter six (second-fourth seal judgments) will start. Once this war commences, shortages to the point of severe starvation will be worldwide.

Water

So let's take a look at some of the general necessities you will need. Water is one of the staples of life. Without clean drinkable water, you would not be able to survive beyond a few days. Since the Bible is clear, at some point during the second half of the tribulation period, the entire fresh water supply will be destroyed or polluted by God, it is advisable that you have access to a water source.

One option is bottled water. Experts estimate bottled water to have a 2-4 year shelf life. The minimum daily amount you will need to store is one gallon per person. That would bring the minimum amount of water you would need to store for a family of four for one year to 1,460 gallons. Multiply that number times 3.5 (years) and the amount of water needed grows to over 5,000 gallons.

This is a tremendous amount of water that will be hard to transport and store. It is more practical to locate your shelter near a freshwater source until it is no longer available. In doing so, you need only purchase a portable water purifier system that guards against impurities, viruses, microbes, pathogens, and disease.

Two highly rated portable water purifiers I recommend are the Katadyn Pocket Water Microfilter and the SteriPEN Traveler Handheld Water Purifier. The Katadyn Pocket Water Microfilter is about the size and shape of a cylinder water bottle (weighs 20 ounces), has a very rugged and durable construction (lifetime warranty), and uses a ceramic filter that can be cleaned several times, even in the field, and purifies up to 13,000 gallons of water per filter. More importantly, the element filters all microorganisms larger than 0.2 microns (0.0002mm), producing clear, drinkable water no matter where in the world you are. To operate, place the input hose into the water source and the output hose into the water container and pump. Absolutely no electric power source is required to operate.

A second level of water purification I would propose is the SteriPEN Traveler Handheld Water Purifier. This portable water purifier is a little bigger than a permanent marker (6.1 inches long) and weighs 3.6 ounces. It works by using ultraviolet light (UV) to destroy the DNA of microorganisms, making them unable to reproduce and cause illness. To operate, just turn the ultraviolet light on and begin stirring the bulb end in a liter of water for about one minute. At the end of the required time, the water is purified for safe consumption. There are two battery operated models. I suggest you purchase the model that uses two CR123 batteries. For every two batteries, you can purify up to 200 liters of water. Since recharging will not be an option you will need to have a supply of disposable batteries available (50 batteries = 1325 gallons of purified water).

I would have at least two of each of these water purifiers with extra replacement parts as part of my survival kit. All associated purifying equipment and parts can easily be transported in a backpack. Make sure you read the instructions for both purifiers thoroughly to prevent cross contamination.

At the time of this writing, these two products were two of the best portable water purifiers on the market, but that could change in time. Make sure you continue to research to ensure that you have the best portable purifiers available. The availability of safe drinking water will be a vital necessity during this time period (see Survival Resources section; selecting a water purifier).

Food, Medicine & Clothing

Food staples with a long shelf life are next on the list. Upon researching different types of food, canned juices, meats (tuna, chicken, ham), vegetables, soups, and fruits had a shelf life of two years and beyond. All canned goods should be low-sodium and stored in a cool place. Virtually all canned goods contain a significant amount of water that can be consumed. There are also many high calorie protein bars on the market that have between a 3-5 year shelf life. Two of the more notable survival bars are the Mayday 2400 and Mainstay 3600. Of course, MREs, flour, white rice, sugar, dried soybeans, and powdered milk, if stored correctly, have long shelf lives (see Survival Resources section; Food Shelf Life Chart).

The caloric daily intake per person ranges from 1,500-2,500 calories a day depending on gender and activity level. You will also have to make certain that your diet includes essential proteins, carbohydrates, and fats. For a family of four you will need to have on hand food that will provide daily 6,000-10,000 nutritional calories.

You will need basic medical supplies (make out a list) along with a long-term supply of any prescription drugs your family members may need over the next 3½ plus years. You will not be able to receive life preserving prescriptions or medical attention of any kind without taking the mark under the new world order. It is possible various Christian underground black market services will be available including stolen prescription drugs and doctors who have refused to take the mark. However, I certainly wouldn't count on it (see Survival Resources section; home medical remedies).

Based on your location and climate, you will need clothing, hats, gloves, footwear, and blankets that will sustain you over the next 3½ years. I would suggest you purchase a -20 F thermal sleeping bag or whatever the best rated bag is at that time. Other supplies that should be included: A Bible (mandatory), eating utensils (can opener), a cranking radio with flashlight, gas mask, hammer axe, saw, knife, sharpener, survival staff, Leatherman multi-tool, zip ties, backpack, waterproof matches or lighters, magnesium flint stick, compass/whistle/ magnifier, a map of area, reading glasses, sewing kit, paracord (1,000 feet min.), fishing equipment, compound bow with arrows, slingshot, and a gun with ammunition. Actually, you should have more than one of some of these items in case of malfunction. Look for equipment that is well built and multi-purpose. Some of these items may change or be upgraded in time but you get the idea. Be sure to seek professional training for weapons use (see Survival Resources section; various links).

Survival Training & Planting Seeds

It would be highly advisable to learn wilderness survival skills such as trapping, hunting, fishing, finding bird eggs, fire starting (without matches/lighter), building a shelter, wilderness medical skills, identifying edible vegetation (for area) and insects, and primitive water purification techniques. As much as possible, survival skills should be based on the area you expect to inhabit. Any learned skills should be taken immediately and practiced regularly to stay sharp. Don't wait for disaster to strike before you try them out. There are plenty of books and videos available to help you learn the skills and identify eatable items.

The same goes for those who plan to purchase seeds to plant for gardening. Plan ahead, know the area you expect to farm, and practice. Growing food from seedlings is not easy and will require much training in advance. Make sure the seed selection you choose will grow well in the area or region you choose.

Some may question whether the land will be suitable for growing food during the final 3½ years of the tribulation period. Scripture does suggest that farming will still be feasible even up to the second coming of Christ. Jesus, describing how He will gather the nations for the judgment to enter the Millennium said, "Then shall two be in the field; the one shall be taken, and the other left. Two women shall be grinding at the mill; the one shall be taken, and the other left (Matthew 24:40-41)." Some incorrectly believe this passage is describing the rapture of the church, but a closer investigation proves otherwise. This gathering will take place following the second coming of Christ or just after the tribulation period is over. The mention of two being in the field (farming) and two women grinding (grain) leads me to believe the condition of the land will still be viable for planting even up to the end of the tribulation.

A great resource for those who plan to grow their own food under survival conditions is *Food Production Systems for a Backyard or Small Farm*. Their system covers many topics including organic survival gardening, seed saving, and water systems to name a few (see Survival Resources section; Beginning Farmer).

Water Sources & Nuclear Fallout

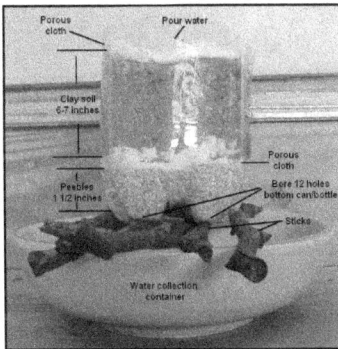

FIGURE 1: EARTH FILTER

There may be those who believe they can live off the land and make it through this period on their survival expertise. That may be possible for some years into the tribulation period, but eventually the plagues God will bring upon the earth will likely destroy virtually all known water sources. Without clean drinkable water, you will be dead within a week.

This can be remedied by learning alternative methods of harvesting water through various plants, trees, and water collection (rain water and morning dew collection) strategies. It is imperative that you know what possible water sources are available in the region you wish to habitat in. Many are not aware that some trees can hold an abundant amount of clean filtered water (banana, bamboo, and cactus).

If you are concerned that your water source may be contaminated by nuclear radiation there is a way to filter it. An effective way to remove most radioactive fallout and dissolved particles in contaminated water is filtering through earth. Oism.org provides detailed instructions on how to create a homemade filtration system from common household items and your natural surroundings.

> Filtering through earth removes essentially all of the fallout particles and more of the dissolved radioactive material than does boiling-water distillation, a generally impractical purification method that does not eliminate dangerous radioactive iodine's. Earth filters are also more effective in removing radioactive iodine's than are ordinary ion-exchange water softeners or charcoal filters. In areas of heavy fallout, about 99% of the radioactivity in

water could be removed by filtering it through ordinary earth.

To make the simple, effective filter shown in [Fig. 1], the only materials needed are those found in and around the home. This expedient filter can be built easily by proceeding as follows:

1. Perforate the bottom of a 5-gallon can, a large bucket, a watertight wastebasket, or a similar container with about a dozen nail holes. Punch the holes from the bottom upward, staying within about 2 inches of the center.

2. Place a layer about 1 inch thick of washed pebbles or small stones on the bottom of the can. If pebbles are not available, twisted coat-hanger wires or small sticks can be used.

3. Cover the pebbles with one thickness of terrycloth towel, burlap sackcloth, or other quite porous cloth. Cut the cloth in a roughly circular shape about 3 inches larger than the diameter of the can.

4. Take soil containing some clay almost any soil will do from at least 4 inches below the surface of the ground. (Nearly all fallout particles

remain near the surface except after deposition on sand or gravel.)

5. Pulverize the soil, then gently press it in layers over the cloth that covers the pebbles, so that the cloth is held snugly against the sides of the can. Do not use pure clay (not porous enough) or sand (too porous). The soil in the can should be 6 to 7 inches thick.

6. Completely cover the surface of the soil layer with one thickness of fabric as porous as a bath towel. This is to keep the soil from being eroded as water is poured into the filtering can. The cloth also will remove some of the particles from the water. A dozen small stones placed on the cloth near its edges will secure it adequately.

7. Support the filter can on rods or sticks placed across the top of a container that is larger in diameter than the filter can. (A dishpan will do.)

The contaminated water should be poured into the filter can, preferably after allowing it to settle as described below. The filtered water should be disinfected by one of the previously described methods.

If the 6 or 7 inches of filtering soil is a sandy clay loam, the filter initially will deliver about 6 quarts of clear water per hour. (If the filtration rate is faster than about 1 quart in 10 minutes, remove the upper fabric and recompress the soil.) After several hours, the rate will be reduced to about 2 quarts per hour.

When the filtering rate becomes too slow, it can be increased by removing and rinsing the surface fabric, removing about 1 inch of soil, and then replacing the fabric. The life of a filter is extended and its efficiency increased if muddy water is first allowed to settle for several hours in a separate container, as described below. After about 50 quarts have been filtered, rebuild the filter by replacing the used soil with fresh soil.

Settling

Settling is one of the easiest methods to remove most fallout particles from water. Furthermore, if the water to be used is muddy or murky, settling it before filtering will extend the life of the filter. The procedure is as follows:

1. Fill a bucket or other deep container three quarters full of the contaminated water.

2. Dig pulverized clay or clayey soil from a depth of four or more inches below ground surface, and stir it into the water. Use about a 1-inch depth of dry clay or dry clayey soil for every 4-inch depth of water. Stir until practically all the clay particles are suspended in the water.

3. Let the clay settle for at least 6 hours. The settling clay particles will carry most of the suspended fallout particles to the bottom and cover them.

4. Carefully dip out or siphon the clear water, and disinfect it.

Settling and Filtering

Although dissolved radioactive material usually is only a minor danger in fallout-contaminated water, it is safest to filter even the clear water produced by settling, if an earth filter is available. Finally as always the water should be disinfected.[1]

For illustration purposes, the plastic bottle used for the earth filter (Fig. 1) was cut short.

---

[1] Wigner, Eugene P. "Ch. 8: Water." *Nuclear War Survival Skills*. Retrieved July 23, 2011 (http://www.oism.org/nwss/s73p919.htm).

You should provide as much space as possible for pouring water into the filter to supply a continuous drip into the purified water reservoir.

Oism.org also provides a few suggestions where one might be able to find hidden uncontaminated water sources in and around the area you are located.

Survivors of a nuclear attack should realize that neither fallout particles nor dissolved radioactive elements or compounds can be removed from water by chemical disinfecting or boiling. Therefore, water should be obtained from the least radioactive sources available. Before a supply of stored drinking water has been exhausted, other sources should be located. The main water sources are given below, with the safest source listed first and the other sources listed in decreasing order of safety.

1. Water from deep wells and from water tanks and covered reservoirs into which no fallout particles or fallout-contaminated water has been introduced. (Caution: Although most spring water would be safe, some spring water is surface water that has flowed into

and through underground channels without having been filtered.)

2. Water from covered seepage pits or shallow, hand-dug wells. This water is usually safe IF fallout or fallout-contaminated surface water has been prevented from entering by the use of waterproof coverings and by waterproofing the surrounding ground to keep water from running down outside the well casing. If the earth is not sandy, gravelly, or too porous, filtration through earth is very effective.

3. Contaminated water from deep lakes. Water from a deep lake would be much less contaminated by dissolved radioactive material and fallout particles than water from a shallow pond would be, if both had the same amount of fallout per square foot of surface area deposited in them. Furthermore, fallout particles settle to the bottom more rapidly in deep lakes than in shallow ponds, which are agitated more by wind.

4. Contaminated water from shallow ponds and other shallow, still water.

5. Contaminated water from streams, which would be especially

dangerous if the stream is muddy from the first heavy rains after fallout is deposited. The first runoff will contain most of the radioactive material that can be dissolved from fallout particles deposited on the drainage area. Runoff after the first few heavy rains following the deposit of fallout is not likely to contain much dissolved radioactive material or fallout.

6. Water collected from fallout-contaminated roofs. This would contain more fallout particles than would the runoff from the ground.

7. Water obtained by melting snow that has fallen through air containing fallout particles, or from snow lying on the ground onto which fallout has fallen. Avoid using such water for drinking or cooking, if possible.[2]

Location

In conclusion, if a person were to locate a secret wilderness hideaway that was beyond the reach of the new world order (Antichrist

---

[2] Wigner, Eugene P. "Ch. 8: Water." *Nuclear War Survival Skills*. Retrieved July 6, 2011 (http://www.oism.org/nwss/s73p919.htm).

40

kingdom), and secure in advance all the necessary food and supplies to survive the final half of the tribulation period, it would take a very large moving truck to transport it, if the truck was even able get to said location. Frankly, staying light and mobile will likely be a big factor in assuring one's survivability during this time period.

FIGURE 2: LOCATION OF PETRA

With this in mind, obtaining skills that would enable you to live off the land seems to be the best survival strategy.

So what does the Bible have to say about location choice during the tribulation period? The only place of refuge the Bible says God promises to protect during this horrible time period is Petra (Fig. 2) located along the southwestern Jordanian-Israeli border. During the second half of the tribulation period, a faithful remnant of Jews will be forced to flee to this ancient rock-hewn cliff city where God will protect and nourish them until He returns in the clouds of glory (Daniel 11:41, Revelation 12:14, Isaiah 63:1).

All others who refuse to take the mark (Christians; Revelation 13:8) will likely spend the final 3½ years living on the run or will face death in Christ (Revelation 15:2). But be encouraged, the Bible is clear that there will be survivors, and by the grace of God, you can be one of them.

I will leave you with advice from Jesus Himself regarding the survivability of this time period found in Matthew 24:15-22:

> When ye therefore shall see the abomination of desolation, spoken of by Daniel the prophet, stand in the holy place, (whoso readeth, let him understand:) then let them which be in Judaea flee into the mountains: Let him which is on the housetop not come down to take anything out of his house: Neither let him which is in the field return back to take his clothes. And woe unto them that are with child, and to them that give suck in those days! But pray ye that your flight be not in the winter, neither on the sabbath day: For then shall be great tribulation, such as was not since the beginning of the world to this time, no, nor ever shall be. And except those days should be shortened, there should no flesh be

saved: but for the elect's sake those days shall be shortened.

This warning from our Lord is directed more toward those in and around Jerusalem, who will see firsthand the Antichrist desecrate the Temple, but still yields sound advice to all who will listen and obey. As the Lord Jesus looks into the future, He describes the day when this Temple desecration takes place. Jesus then says, when you see this happen, drop what you are doing and flee to the mountains. When this event takes place, all time for preparation will be over. Now is the time to put into action any plan you may have.

I believe this is a survival tip from Jesus Himself. Not only is He giving Jews of that day a glimpse into the future, He also provides future Christians with advance warning when and where to flee.

This isn't the first time Jesus has given a prophetic warning regarding future events. In Luke 21:20-21, He provided a peek into what would be the future destruction of Israel (70 AD) with a little advice attached. He states, "And when ye shall see Jerusalem compassed with armies, then know that the desolation thereof is nigh. Then let them which are in Judaea flee to the mountains; and let them which are in the midst of it depart out; and let not them that are in the countries enter thereinto."

Some forty years later, Roman General Vespasian surrounded Jerusalem (just as Jesus prophesied), and would have overthrown the city, but was called back to Rome due to the sudden death of Emperor Nero. When the siege was lifted, Jews who were believers in Jesus remembered His prophetic warning, heeded His advice, and fled to the mountains. Titus, son of Vespasian, later returned and burned the city to the ground, but not one Christian who heeded the warning of Jesus was killed. It would be wise to apply this as fundamental advice for our present generation as well wherever you may live.

While researching survival locations, I found that experts agreed with Scripture and felt mountain survival living provided good potential sources of water (snow, streams, etc.), food, and shelter. It also proved to be difficult terrain for search parties and a good hiding place for those who desired to stay hidden from civilization. But if one is to survive in this difficult environment they will need to seek out advanced mountain training skills.

An ideal place to acquire such skills is at the Boulder Outdoor Survival School headquartered in Boulder, Colorado. They specialize in ultra-light travel through mountains and canyons and surviving with little more than a blanket, poncho, and a knife. However, this course is not designed for your typical couch potato. You will need to be in shape before you begin the course.

Certainly, it is highly advisable that you immediately begin a proper diet and exercise program the minute you realize the rapture has taken place. This will play an important part in maintaining your health, strength, and durability in the trying days ahead. For more survival tips and information, here is a website called Survival Outdoor Skills. This survival website is loaded with great tips and information (see Survival Resources section; various links).

Of course, you can avoid the unspeakable horrors of the tribulation period by coming to Christ, repenting of your sins, acknowledging Him as Savior, and turning your life over to Him. It is only through Christ Jesus that we can obtain eternal life and be assured of our heavenly destination. I encourage you to make that commitment to Jesus today.

If the rapture has already taken place, you can still come to the Lord. It's not too late! However, you will still have to face the terrors of the seven-year tribulation period.

How Much Time Will Transpire Between The Rapture And The Beginning Of The Seven-Year Tribulation?

There will be 75 days (Daniel 12:11-13) between the second coming of Christ and the beginning of the millennial Reign of Christ. I would think that Satan would at least need that much time to figure out he is now unopposed and choose his Antichrist and false prophet. But truthfully, it could be years between the rapture and the start of the tribulation period. If Jesus will take 75 days transitioning from the second coming of Christ to the start of the Millennium you can bet it will take at least that much time for Satan to set up his kingdom. In my opinion, it is highly unlikely the tribulation period will begin immediately following the rapture of the church.

Wars Of The Tribulation Period

The Bible says there are many wars still yet to play out until the end of the tribulation period. Some that will be listed could take place simultaneously or be separate wars altogether. Some may take place before the tribulation period begins and others during this horrible time period. It is very important that you are aware of when they may take place and what parts of the world they will affect. Here is a list of these future prophetic Biblical wars and when they may occur.

Psalm 83 War

It's hard to say when the Psalm 83 war will commence. I tend to believe that the nations listed in Psalm 83 are just an extension of the Battle of Gog and Magog described in Ezekiel 38 & 39. According to this passage, this war will include the following biblical nations: Edom, the Ishmaelites, Moab, the Hagrites,

Gebal, Ammon, Amalek, Philistia, Tyre, and Assyria.

Bill Salus, author of the book *Isralestine*, narrows these modern-day countries down to Hezbollah, Syria, Egypt, Saudi Arabia, Jordan, Hamas and the Palestinians.[3] I agree that these nations will be involved in this future war. However, many of these biblical lands listed in Psalm 83 can be interpreted to include virtually all of the nations that will be involved in the Battle of Gog and Magog.

For this reason, I tend to believe that the Psalm 83 War will take place in connection with the Battle of Gog and Magog. There are those who believe this war could happen before or after the rapture takes place.

The prevailing view is that this war will take place just prior to the Battle of Gog and Magog. It will be confined to the Middle East region but will likely set off a spike in oil prices and a major drop in financial markets around the world.

The Destruction of Damascus

Many in the world of prophecy believe the Bible speaks of a day when Damascus will be completely destroyed never to be inhabited

---

[3] Salus, Bill. 2008. *Isralestine*. Crane, MO: Anomalos Publishing, 20.

again. Here is the Scripture verse that points to this longstanding prophecy:

"The burden of Damascus. Behold, Damascus is taken away from being a city, and it shall be a ruinous heap (Isaiah 17:1)."

Damascus, Syria is the oldest continuously inhabited city in the world. To date, this prophecy has never been fulfilled. When will this prophecy finally come to pass?

As stated previously, many believe Syria will play a major role in the Psalm 83 War. When this war commences, it is very likely a Syrian controlled Hezbollah will begin their SCUD missile barrage on the cities of Israel. Israel has warned Syria, if Hezbollah attacks them, they will hold Syria responsible. I suspect, at the beginning of the Psalm 83 war, Hezbollah will begin launching their very powerful and accurate SCUD missiles on Israel's capital Tel Aviv. Combined with all the other simultaneous attacks, Israel may see this as an existential threat and decide to launch a nuclear counterstrike against Damascus thus reducing it to rubble.

Battle of Gog and Magog

In the last days, it is predicted in Ezekiel 38 & 39, Russia, and an Islamic coalition will rise up and attack Israel. Many of these nations are enemies of Israel today. Listed are Iran, Ethiopia, Libya, Sudan, and Turkey. It wouldn't surprise me if the nations listed in Psalm 83 were also involved.

It isn't completely clear when this attack will occur. It's possible it could take place before the tribulation period begins, during the gap of time between the rapture and the start of the tribulation or during the tribulation period. I lean toward the beginning of the tribulation period.

This prophesied attack will be based on greed, control of the Middle East, and/or to challenge the authority of the Antichrist (if the battle takes place during the tribulation). The Islamic world will take part in this battle for the sole purpose of finally wiping Israel off the face of the map.

Russia and its allies will launch a twofold attack, by land and by air from the north. Sudan, Libya, and Ethiopia will come in from the south with its military arsenal while Turkey and Iran will cover the remaining theaters of operation. It is believed that this attack will be a complete surprise to Israel. But as the northern armies reach the mountains of Israel something supernatural will occur. As described in Ezekiel 38:14-22, God will rise up and completely destroy the invading Islamic and Russian forces. His method of destruction...He will rain fire and brimstone down from heaven. This will destroy every jetfighter in the air. At the same time, God will cause a great earthquake to occur that will shake the entire world. This will destroy and dismantle all armored vehicles and cause major casualties on the ground. For those who survive the earthquake, He will then cause mass confusion amongst the armies and they will begin to kill each other. The Book of Ezekiel further states that those that are not killed in the previous three ways will be killed by plagues, wild animals, and plain old fear. Simply put, they'll be scared to death.

Eighty-three percent of the invading army will die in the mountains of Israel in the worst military defeat in history. It will take 7 months to bury the dead (Ezekiel 39:12) and Israel will burn the weapons left behind for 7 years (Ezekiel 39:9).

It is my belief, following this great and miraculous defeat, many in the Islamic world will convert to the true God, but not without a cost. It is likely a great worldwide revival will follow this war (Ezekiel 38:23).

The Apocalypse

When the second seal is opened it reveals a red horse and rider (Revelation 6:3-4). This illustrates that peace will be removed from the earth and open conflict will break out everywhere. This war will take place during the tribulation period and likely just before the midway point.

Of course, we have seen war throughout history, and even today, it is a constant threat worldwide. However, in that day, this war will be unparallel to anything that has ever happened in the past. God will allow this to take place as part of His judgment upon the earth.

Although the Antichrist will come in peace, his plans will see resistance and worldwide war will break out. It isn't known which nations will take part in this war, but they will be no match for the armies of the Antichrist and will be soundly defeated. The Bible says one-quarter of the world's population will be killed as a result of this war (Revelation 6:8). It is possible that the Psalm 83 War, the destruction of Damascus, and the Battle of Gog and Magog could take place as part of this great war. Given the death toll, I would have to believe that nuclear weapons will be used and Israel's enemies will take this opportunity to finally destroy them. However, both the kingdom of the Antichrist and Israel will survive.

Crushing victory after victory by the Antichrist will cause the nations of the world to fear and tremble. Many will be mesmerized by his accomplishments and the speed of his ascension. But the damage from the many wars will be staggering and many of the effects will be irreversible. Eventually, he will require the world to worship him and they will (Revelation 13:4).

It should also be noted, although Israel will survive this devastating world war, the Antichrist will later declare war on the Jewish nation forcing many to flee. Most prophecy teachers believe they will seek refuge in the ancient city of Petra.

This brings up a very good question. Most Military experts project that Israel has a minimum of 80 nuclear weapons. Why wouldn't Israel use their nuclear arsenal against the invading armies of the Antichrist? Certainly, this would be considered an existential threat. My guess is the Apocalypse will completely deplete Israel of all their nuclear weapons reducing their military to a conventional weapons level. With the armies of the world at his command, the Antichrist will easily conquer Israel and set up his throne.

Subduing of Three Kings

The Bible says the Antichrist will rise to power out of a ten nation alliance who will lend him their power for a short time period (Daniel 7:24; Revelation 17:12-17). Apparently, there will be a power struggle among the ten nations and three will have to be brought under subjection. Most Bible prophecy experts believe the Antichrist will rise up out of the European Union. Today, there are three predominant nations that rule the EU...France, Germany, and the UK. These three nations may represent the prophesied kings that the Antichrist will subdue. I can't imagine how many people will die during this war but I'm sure the number will be staggering. This war could take place during the Antichrist's rise to power, the Apocalypse or after he declares himself to be

God. Upon his declaration to be a god, these three countries may see him as a potential Hitler.

The War Against the Jews and Christians

Toward the latter half of the tribulation period, the Antichrist and the world will wage war against the Jews and those who become Christians during this time period. Prophecy expert Dr. David Reagan describes it as a vicious attack by Satan and another Holocaust:

> There is going to be another holocaust during the latter half of the Tribulation. When Satan is cast down to earth, he will possess the Antichrist (Revelation 13:2) and inspire him to annihilate all the Jews. This is the reason that Jesus referred to the last half of the Tribulation as "the great tribulation" (Matthew 24:21) — not because this half will be worse than the first half, but because the wrath of Satan will be focused on the Jews.
>
> Zechariah 13:8 indicates that two-thirds of the Jewish people will be killed by the Antichrist during this time, and Revelation 12:17 says the Antichrist will also war against the "offspring" of Israel — namely, those "who keep the commandments of God and hold to the testimony of

Jesus." I believe this is a reference to all those who accept Jesus as their Lord and Savior during the Tribulation, both Jews and Gentiles.[4]

The Bible says that Satan's war against those who receive Jesus Christ during the tribulation will be very successful as evidenced by the great host of martyrs in heaven (Revelation 7:9-14). It is possible this great persecution could begin following the Battle of Gog & Magog. The Bible says the purpose of this great battle will be an opportunity for God to magnify Himself in the eyes of the nations. The result, "I [God] will be known in the eyes of many nations, and they shall know that I am the LORD (Ezekiel 38:23)."

It is my belief, many in the Moslem world will turn to the Lord following this miraculous victory and will be killed for their conversion.

This worldwide martyrdom will continue throughout the remainder of the tribulation period. It is generally believed by prophecy experts that Christians will become wanted fugitives to be hunted down and killed. This

---

[4] Reagan, David R. "Wars Of The End Times: How Many And When They Will Happen?" *Lamb & Lion Ministries.* Retrieved April 23, 2011 (http://www.lamblion.com/articles/articles_tribulation1.php).

global martyrdom could begin as early as two years into the tribulation period.

The Destruction Of Mystery Babylon

During the tribulation period there will be a nation that will rule over the Antichrist and his ten-nation kingdom (Revelation 17:1-18). This nation, known as Mystery Babylon, will dictate what the Antichrist can and cannot do for the first half of the tribulation period. They will be a formidable dynasty of this time.

Not only will they have great worldwide political power, they'll also be very wealthy and religious in nature. Notice in the description (Revelation 17:1-18), Mystery Babylon is pictured as a harlot riding a beast (Antichrist). The beast is described as having ten horns (revived Roman Empire) representing ten nations, which are subject to the beast. In essence, Mystery Babylon has given the beast and the ten nations their power, but remains very much in control. This will change toward the middle of the tribulation period.

At around the middle of the tribulation period, after Satan is defeated and removed from heaven, he will enter (possess) the Antichrist. This will start the beginning of the end for Mystery Babylon. For Satan would not be ruled over by God, and will not tolerate being ruled over by man either. God, at this time, will use the Antichrist and his kingdom to exact judgment upon this wicked nation.

> And the ten horns which thou
> sawest upon the beast, these shall
> hate the whore, and shall make her
> desolate and naked, and shall eat
> her flesh, and burn her with fire.
> For God hath put in their hearts to
> fulfill his will, and to agree, and
> give their kingdom unto the beast,
> until the words of God shall be
> fulfilled (Revelation 17:16, 17).

The Antichrist and his kingdom will turn on
Mystery Babylon and launch an all-out nuclear
attack. The destruction from a Mystery Babylon
counter attack is not mentioned, but I'm sure
there will be casualties. Not only is Mystery
Babylon defeated, the destruction is so
dreadful that the land is no longer fit for use or
to inhabit (Revelation 18:15-23).

The defeat of this superpower nation is so swift
and decisive it will leave the rest of the world
terrified and shocked. For this was the greatest
nation on the face of the earth and in one hour
they have been completely destroyed. Kings,
dignitaries, and businessmen are all left
wondering what will happen next as they
scramble to recoup losses and position
themselves for what may happen with this
dramatic change of power.

This war will likely commence around the
midway point of the tribulation period. The
identity of Mystery Babylon is unknown,
however some have speculated it could be the

US, Rome, New York City or a rebuilt Babylon (Iraq) to name a few.

Kings of East March

At the end of the tribulation period, the kings of the East will march toward Israel with an army of 200 million strong. During their march, the Bible says they will kill one-third of the remaining men on Earth (Revelation 9:15-21). Some believe, given their description, this army could be demon possessed or an army of demons. Their march will start sometime during the second half of the tribulation period and lead them across much of Asia concluding at the Battle of Armageddon (Revelation 19:11-21).

Battle of Armageddon

At the end of the tribulation period, the Lord will gather the nations of the world together for His final triumph. He will descend with all the Saints of God at the second coming of Christ to finally put down all earthly kingdoms. The human army will embody those who have pledged their allegiance to the beast and have taken his mark. Both rich and poor, bond and free, great and small will participate in this battle; however, it will be over before it starts. The Bible says, with the sound of the Lord's voice, their bodies will rot where they stand (Zechariah 14:12). In fact, it is described as a great winepress in which Christ literally crushes His foes and their blood will flow approximately four feet high and two hundred miles long. The slaughter will be so enormous that God will call the birds of the air to come and gorge themselves on the flesh of men (Revelation 19:11-19).

Mark Of The Antichrist 666: How To Positively Identify It When It Does Come

For some reason, there seems to be a great fear by many Christians that they could accidentally take the mark or somehow be tricked into doing so. What most people fail to understand is that this is not about some high tech mark but about a man who will claim to be God and force the world to worship him. This mark is merely an identifying symbol that you must accept or face isolation from the known world and/or death. The mark (666) will be forced upon mankind at the midway point of the tribulation period by the Antichrist.

Certainly, we should be aware of the various devices that are available to make the mark feasible. However, you're not going to wake up one morning to find out that the nifty plastic decoder ring you took out of the box of cereal and wear proudly has been revealed on the news as a symbol of your pledge to the Antichrist. According to the Bible, there are a number of things that must happen first before the mark is put in place on a global scale...many of them supernatural.

Here is a series of events taken straight from the Bible that must happen before the mark can be introduced and actually mandated as international law:

1. The Antichrist must march into the Jerusalem Temple and declare himself to be God (Daniel 9:27; II Thessalonians 2:3-12).

2. The Antichrist will demand worship from the whole world and he will receive it (Revelation 13:8).

3. The false prophet, the Antichrist's high priest, will perform wondrous signs causing lightening to come down from the sky, along with other miracles (Revelation 13:11-14).

4. The false prophet will erect a statue of the Antichrist and make it speak (Revelation 13:14-15).

5. When the statue of the beast speaks, he will demand that everyone must worship the Antichrist and take his mark either on their forehead or on their right hand (Revelation 13:15-17).

6. Whoever does not take this mark will not be able to buy or sell (Revelation 13:17).

7. Before anyone actually takes the mark, God will send out angels throughout the world proclaiming from the sky not to take the mark of the beast but to worship God. The same angels will also proclaim the punishment for

taking the mark...being cast alive into the lake of fire for an eternity (Revelation 14:9-11).

According to the literal Word of God, these 7 events must take place before the worldwide mark of the beast can be distributed by the Antichrist. As stated, these 7 events will happen sometime around the middle of the tribulation period and one right after another. It should also be noted that it wouldn't make any sense for God to send out angels to warn the world of the mark if some had already taken it. You will be granted ample and thorough warnings that cannot be mistaken. One interesting fact is, we can't even get past event number one without the rebuilding of the Jerusalem temple.

Something else I find interesting regarding the mark is found in Revelation 13:17.

"And that no man might buy or sell, save he that had the mark, or the name of the beast, or the number of his name."

This passage lists three possibilities for the mark. 1) It may just be a mark, 2) it may be the name of the beast, or 3) it may be the number of his name which is 666. Certainly, it doesn't really matter. Either you have the identification mark or you don't. It need not be complicated, but due to our fast paced technological society, we feel somehow that it must be. I'm not saying that it won't turn out to be some advanced verichip hybrid, but whatever it is, God will make it clear to every soul on earth that taking the mark of the Antichrist will have severe and eternal consequences (Revelation 14:9-11).

So, according to the Bible, it will not be possible for a person to mistakenly take or be fooled into taking the mark of the beast. It will be your choice, and you will absolutely know all the facts and consequences associated with making such a decision.

You will also have to witness a multitude of supernatural events before you have to confront the decision of whether or not to take the mark of the Antichrist.

Seven Events That Could Quickly Follow The Rapture Of The Church

At this point, we have learned about the rapture of the church and some of the events of the tribulation period. However, what events are most likely to take place directly following the rapture?

There could be a gap of time that could come between the rapture and the start of the tribulation period. You can bet there will be a considerable amount of pandemonium and chaos the likes of which the world has never known. But once the shock of the rapture has subsided these next 7 events could quickly follow.

First, the appearance of the Antichrist who will confirm a seven-year peace agreement with Israel. This agreement will include Israel with many other nations (Daniel 9:25-27). It's likely that Israel will be the centerpiece of this agreement and will serve to bring them world recognition and immediate favored nation status.

This peace accord will probably coincide with a Middle East peace agreement or it may be the agreement in totality. It might even include an incentive for Israel to make peace with the Arab world. I lean toward this theory. It will probably include Palestinian statehood, land concessions, and the promise of sharing Jerusalem as a capital for both Israel and Palestine. Although, in the past, I have included the rebuilding of the Jewish temple as part of the peace agreement, I now have doubts. That will be covered further in the fifth event.

Second, the appearance of the false prophet. Most prophecy teachers and experts tend to focus on the Antichrist failing to mention that the false prophet will probably come to power at the same time. When Satan chooses his Antichrist, he will at this time choose his false prophet. Whether he turns out to be the Pope or some other world religious leader is unimportant. When the Antichrist takes over the world, the false prophet will be standing by his side promoting him and performing mighty wonders (Revelation 13:11-17).

Third, the appearance of God's two witnesses (Revelation 11:3-13). It is generally believed that the two witnesses will come on the scene at the same time the Antichrist and false prophet do. It will be through these two men (whoever they may be) that God will begin spreading the Gospel.

When the two witnesses do come, their ministry will center on Jerusalem. I believe they will be responsible for starting a great revival that will see at least 144,000 Jews saved in the early days of the tribulation period (Revelation 7:4-8). These 144,000 Jews will in turn be sealed by God and sent throughout the world to preach the Gospel. Many will come to know the Lord during this time and most will die for that privilege (Revelation 6:9-11; 7:9-17).

Fourth, the attack on Israel by Russia and the Islamic world (Ezekiel 38 & 39). It's possible that this could occur before the beginning of the tribulation period but more likely it will take place after it starts.

Scripture declares that the reason for their attack will be to take a spoil (Ezekiel 38:4, 11-12), and at the time of this attack, Israel will be dwelling safely and at rest (Ezekiel 38:11). This leads me to believe that they could already be at peace with the Islamic world, but not necessarily with the Antichrist. That agreement could come later in the form of E.U. membership, but it's most probable that they will be at peace with both at the time of the attack.

Fifth, the third Jewish Temple must be rebuilt (Matthew 24:15; II Thessalonians 2:4; Revelation 11:1). In the past, I have stated that the Temple would be rebuilt as part of the agreement with the Antichrist. I'm not so sure that's the case anymore. My main concern is that it is generally believed that no Muslim would ever allow such a sacred site to be desecrated by a Jewish Temple. It would be an unthinkable atrocity and simply would not even enter their minds. This would start a worldwide Muslim holy war.

It is more likely, after Israel's stunning victory over the Russian-Islamic Alliance, that no one will dare stop them. For the whole world will see this victory as a miracle from God (Ezekiel 38:18-23) and shake in fear. That's why I believe the temple will probably be rebuilt 6 months to 2 years after the start of the tribulation period.

Sixth, the Ark of the Covenant will be revealed. After this stunning victory over the Russian-Islamic Alliance, Israel will rush to rebuild their Temple. It is at this time that the Ark of the Covenant will finally be revealed. I am convinced that scripture supports that the Ark of the Covenant will be used during the tribulation period but forgotten when Christ comes to rule and reign on the earth for one thousand years.

A reader of mine brought this verse to my attention:

> And it shall come to pass, when ye be multiplied and increased in the land, in those days, saith the LORD, they shall say no more, the ark of the covenant of the LORD: neither shall it come to mind: neither shall they remember it; neither shall they visit it; neither shall that be done any more (Jeremiah 3:16).

This verse speaks of the Millennium when Jesus will rule and reign for one thousand years. Of course, this is future, but what caught my attention was the portion of the scripture that stated (speaking of the Ark) "neither shall it come to mind: neither shall they remember it; neither shall they visit it; neither shall that be done any more."

I realize that in the context of the entire chapter many interpret this verse to mean that Israel will forget the memory of the Ark of the Covenant when the Lord comes back to rule the earth. But is it possible that it could be foretelling the revealing of the Ark of the Covenant in the last days (tribulation period/rebuilding of the temple) just before the Lord's coming?

Seventh, the Antichrist will put down or subdue three nations (Daniel 7:22-24). Although remote, it's possible that this could occur before the tribulation period during the Antichrist's rise to power.

I believe there will be a space of time between the rapture and the beginning of the tribulation period. During this time, Satan will be free to work out his plan and build his kingdom (Holy Spirit will be removed-II Thessalonians 2:2-11)...he may have to subdue a few nations to accomplish his will. But it's more likely that Daniel is speaking of this happening sometime toward the midway point of the tribulation period. There may be an uprising when the Antichrist declares himself to be God (Revelation 13). These three nations (along with others outside the E.U.) may see him as another potential Hitler.

Part 2:
First Half Of The Tribulation Period

The Tribulation Period Begins

The tribulation period will start with the confirming or signing of a peace accord with the Antichrist, Israel and many nations (Daniel 9:27). This will be a time of unprecedented suffering, the likes of which the world has never experienced. Although the first part of the tribulation period will be difficult, many prophecy scholars believe the real suffering will take place in the latter 3½ years.

The tribulation period is broken up into three separate judgment categories (seal, trumpet, and bowl) with each consisting of 7 individual judgments.

The First Seal Is Now Opened

> And I saw when the Lamb opened one of the seals, and I heard, as it were the noise of thunder, one of the four beasts saying, Come and see. And I saw, and behold a white horse: and he that sat on him had a bow; and a crown was given unto him: and he went forth conquering, and to conquer (Revelation 6:1-2).

Our attention turns toward heaven as the Lord opens the first seal. This reveals a white horse and rider. The rider is the Antichrist. His official appearance will bring about a peace accord with Israel and mark day one of the tribulation period. The Antichrist will come on the scene as a man of peace. When war seems to be breaking out everywhere, he will sway the nations with his charisma, savvy and political charm. He will attempt to fix the world's social, financial and conflict problems (Daniel 8:23-25). In order to accomplish this, he will go forth conquering, taking some nations by force. No one will be able to stand in his way. However, initially, he will come in the name of peace and prosperity.

The first thing that will take place will be a formation of the revived Roman Empire. He will begin by controlling a ten nation block, in which three nations he will take by force (Daniel 7:24). This alliance will be very successful both economically and politically. Many believe the European Union will be this powerful bloc of nations.

The Bible says, this federation of ten separate kings, will bring their kingdoms under the authority of the head of the empire (Revelation 17:12-14). It was through this kingdom (Rome) that Satan unknowingly crucified Christ almost two thousand years ago bringing salvation to all that would accept it. He again, will revive this empire to its former glory to wage war against the Lord.

God's Witnesses

> And I will give power unto my two witnesses, and they shall prophesy a thousand two hundred and

threescore days, clothed in sackcloth. These are the two olive trees, and the two candlesticks standing before the God of the earth. And if any man will hurt them, fire proceedeth out of their mouth, and devoureth their enemies: and if any man will hurt them, he must in this manner be killed. These have power to shut heaven, that it rain not in the days of their prophecy: and have power over waters to turn them to blood, and to smite the earth with all plagues, as often as they will (Revelation 11:3-6).

Although God has raptured His church, He will eventually have many witnesses to tell the world the Truth. These witnesses will come in three different forms, one, the angels (Revelation 14:6-11); two, the 144,000 Jewish witnesses (Revelation 7); and three, the two witnesses from God (Revelation 11:3-8).

The two witnesses will come on the scene at the beginning of the tribulation period. There has been much speculation regarding the two witnesses and their identities. I believe they will be Moses and Elijah, who appeared with Jesus at the transfiguration (Matthew 17:3).

Their message will be one of repentance, judgment and preparation for the coming King. They will preach on the streets of Jerusalem and be dressed in sackcloth. Their ministry will last the first 3½ years of the tribulation and they will be responsible for a great revival breaking out in Israel.

Because of their Gospel message and supernatural power many will seek to kill them. Although many the world over will try, no one will be able to harm them. They will be given special powers to kill their enemies with fire or whatever means their enemies attempt to kill them. They will have the power to stop the rain from falling, turn water to blood, call fire down from heaven, and bring massive plagues on the earth. Anyone who attempts to stop them from fulfilling their earthly ministry will be literally destroyed. No man or army will be able to stop or hinder their mission, not even the Antichrist.

Yes, both the Antichrist and the Lord's two witnesses will be on the scene at the same time. However, at the conclusion of the first half of the tribulation period, God will allow them to be killed by the Antichrist. It should be mentioned, when they are killed, a worldwide celebration, along with the exchanging of gifts, will take place "because these two prophets tormented them that dwelt on the earth (Revelation 11:10)."

The second group of witnesses, the 144,000 Jews, will come out of this great revival in Israel. They will be set aside to preach the message of salvation to the entire world and will be protected by God. Many will be saved during their ministry as stated in Revelation 7:9-17. Their mission will virtually last the entire 7 years of the tribulation period. The Bible makes a point that all 144,000 witnesses will be male Jews who will be virgins (Revelation 14:3-4).

The third group of witnesses are angels. During the course of the tribulation period, angels will visibly appear in the sky preaching to the inhabitants of the earth. Their message will be of repentance and warning not to take the mark of the beast (Revelation 14:6-11).

The Second Seal Is Opened

> And when he had opened the second seal, I heard the second beast say, come and see. And there went out another horse that was red: and power was given to him that sat thereon to take peace from the earth, and that they should kill one another: and there was given unto him a great sword (Revelation 6:3-4).

When the second seal is opened it reveals a red horse and rider. This illustrates that peace will be removed from the earth. Of course, we have seen war throughout history, and even today, it is a constant threat worldwide. However, in that day, this will be a war that will be unparallel to anything that has happened in the past. God will allow this to take place as part of His judgment upon the earth.

Although the Antichrist will come in peace, his plans will see resistance and worldwide war will break out. It isn't known which nations will take part in this war, but they will be no match for the Antichrist and will be soundly defeated.

This victory by the Antichrist will cause the nations to fear and tremble. Many will be mesmerized by his accomplishments and the speed of his ascension. Life will definitely be changed forever from that day forward.

Following this great world war, the Antichrist will likely set up his headquarters in Rome. In time, this will become both the political and religious capital of the world. It is my belief that the world religions will unite under one religious order and exercise great political influence for the first 3½ years. However, at the beginning of the second half of the tribulation, the false prophet will rise up out of this false religious order and betray her.

If I were to predict how far into the tribulation period we are when this war breaks out, I would say about 2 or 3 years.

The Third Seal Is Broken

> And when he had opened the third seal, I heard the third beast say, Come and see. And I beheld, and lo

a black horse; and he that sat on him had a pair of balances in his hand. And I heard a voice in the midst of the four beasts say, A measure of wheat for a penny, and three measures of barley for a penny; and see thou hurt not the oil and the wine (Revelation 6:5-6).

After the third seal is opened a black horse and rider with balances will appear. This indicates that a great famine worldwide will occur on the earth. The effects of no rain and plagues by the two witnesses will only magnify the situation. The devastation of war will produce disease and hunger. Only one tenth of the normal food supply will be available. Many will suffer starvation. Others will steal to survive. It would not surprise me if strict rationing legislation were passed internationally, and the death penalty imposed for anyone caught stealing. These will be desperate times and certainly a time of lawlessness.

The warning "see thou hurt not the oil and the wine" is emphasized in verse 6. This indicates that even though the poor will be at starvation levels, the famine won't have the same effect on those who are wealthy.

The Fourth Seal Is Broken

And when he had opened the fourth seal, I heard the voice of the fourth

> beast say, Come and see. And I looked, and behold a pale horse: and his name that sat on him was Death, and Hell followed with him. And power was given unto them over the fourth part of the earth, to kill with sword, and with hunger, and with death, and with the beasts of the earth (Revelation 6:7-8).

The fourth seal is broken and reveals an ashen horse and rider coming on the scene. The rider has been given the name of Death. Through this great world war one-quarter of the world's population will be killed. Taking into consideration that today's world population is almost 8 billion, it can be assumed almost 2 billion people will die.

Although the Antichrist will come in peace, his agenda will be met through much bloodshed. When his peace plan does fail, the offenders will be exterminated. But the world will view his brutal military action as a necessary evil to attain the ultimate goal of world peace. Hunger will also claim a great many lives. However, the most frightening death of all will not be human. In that day, literally millions of people will be killed by wild beast. It appears God will take away the fear of man from animals. What used to be prey will now became predator.

Just imagine yourself coming home from work. As you drive up to your house, the family pet comes running out to greet you, so you think. Little do you know, he's already killed everyone in the house. As you reach down to pet him, he leaps and knocks you to the ground. Something has gone terribly wrong. Suddenly, other vicious pets in the neighborhood come and join in on the kill. You struggle, but to no avail. One has you by the throat while the others are tearing you apart. The only thing left to do is die.

Russia And Their Allies Attack Israel

It isn't completely clear when this attack will occur. It is possible that it could take place before the tribulation period begins, during the gap of time between the rapture and the start of the tribulation or during the tribulation period. I lean toward the beginning of the tribulation.

If it occurs during the tribulation period Israel will be under the protection of the Antichrist, through the guidelines of his peace plan. Although the Antichrist will probably be the head of the European Union, with powerful allies, not all nations will bend their knee to his authority. In fact, some will even challenge his authority. One of these countries will be Russia.

It is predicted in Ezekiel 38 and 39, in what is known as the Battle of Gog and Magog, Russia and an Islamic alliance will attack Israel. Many of these nations are enemies of Israel today. Listed are Iran, Ethiopia, Libya, Sudan, and Turkey. It wouldn't surprise me if the nations listed in Psalm 83 (Hezbollah, Syria, Egypt, Saudi Arabia, Jordan, Hamas and the Palestinians) were also involved.

This prophesied attack will be based on greed, control of the Middle East, and/or to challenge the authority of the Antichrist (if it takes place during the tribulation). The Islamic world will take part for the sole purpose of finally wiping Israel off the face of the map. Russia, on the other hand, will likely attack to possess Israel's future oil riches.

Though many around the world will see this as an opportunity to destroy Israel something miraculous will take place. Just before Russia and their allies attack, God will supernaturally destroy this great army. His weapons of choice...pestilences, earthquakes, fire and brimstone, driving rain and great hailstones (Ezekiel 38:21-22). By the time this battle is over, the Russian-Islamic Alliance will have been soundly defeated and will lose 83% of their military.

The Bible says the whole world will be stunned and amazed over this great victory, against insurmountable odds, and give glory to God (Ezekiel 38:23).

The Antichrist Is Gaining Power

We are now about 3 or 3½ years into the tribulation period. Up to this point, the Antichrist has brought peace to the Middle East and has put down several foes who have opposed his peace plan. Apparently, there will be a power struggle amongst the ten nations and three will have to be brought under subjection (Daniel 7:24).

Many will die to accomplish the goals of the Antichrist, but considering the world turmoil, death and disasters, things seem to be getting better. The world is now looking to him to solve the hunger problem. After all, he is the head of a very prosperous league of nations, and for a short time, I believe he will bring things under control. However, this will only be the calm before the storm.

The Fifth Seal Is Broken

And when he had opened the fifth seal, I saw under the altar the souls of them that were slain for the word of God, and for the testimony which they held: And they cried with a loud voice, saying, How long, O Lord, holy and true, dost thou not judge and avenge our blood on them that dwell on the earth? And white robes were given unto every one of them; and it was said unto them, that they should rest yet for a little season, until their fellowservants also and their brethren, that should be killed as they were, should be fulfilled (Revelation 6:9-11).

The fifth seal is now broken and the scene shifts to heaven. A host of martyrs are seen in heaven before God. They have been dressed in white signifying their total redemption. Who are these people? They are individuals who have heard the Word and have accepted it. They have been slain for the Word of God that lives in them and their testimony. As in the days of the early church, severe persecution of God's witnesses will be the rule. Many will die for their faith.

Even after all the destruction, devastation, death and famine, those of the earth will not repent. Instead they will slaughter the very ones God has sent to preach the truth. Immediately, upon death, they will be ushered up to heaven. Standing before the throne they are puzzled why God does not immediately destroy these murderers. They are asked to be patient until certain others have been martyred. But He promises that their day of vengeance will come.

Another point that comes to mind is, although religion will flourish during the tribulation period, it will be a Christ-less religious system. I think it is safe to say, at this point in the tribulation period, all indications suggest that God will be considered an enemy of those on the earth.

Satan Is Cast Out Of Heaven

> And there was war in heaven: Michael and his angels fought against the dragon; and the dragon fought and his angels, and prevailed not; neither was their place found any more in heaven. And the great dragon was cast out, that old serpent, called the Devil, and Satan, which deceiveth the whole world: he was cast out into the earth, and his angels were cast out with him (Revelation 12:7-9).

At the beginning of the final 3½ years of the tribulation period, war breaks out in heaven between Satan and his demons, and Christ and His angels. Michael the archangel leads the heavenly host into battle. The result of the battle is to be expected, Satan and his army are soundly defeated.

As a result, Satan and his demons are then cast out of heaven onto the earth. At this point, Satan will know that his time is very short and will be out to destroy everything in his path. The earth will be his new battle ground. His main target will be the nation of Israel and the multitude who will convert to Christianity during the tribulation period. This will begin the most horrible portion of the tribulation period.

> And when the dragon saw that he was cast unto the earth, he persecuted the woman which brought forth the man child. And to the woman were given two wings of a great eagle, that she might fly into the wilderness, into her place, where she is nourished for a time, and times, and half a time, from the face of the serpent. And the serpent cast out of his mouth water as a flood after the woman, that he might cause her to be carried away of the flood. And the earth helped the woman, and the earth opened her mouth, and swallowed up the flood which the dragon cast out of his mouth. And the dragon was wroth with the woman, and went to make war with the remnant of her seed, which keep the commandments of God, and have the testimony of Jesus Christ (Revelation 12:13-17).

With Satan and his army confined to earth, demon possession will be rampant worldwide. Some Bible prophecy experts believe the entire 200 million man army from the East will be demon possessed (Revelation 9:13-19).

Part 3:
Second Half Of The Tribulation Period

The Beginning Of The Second Half Of The Tribulation Period

And when they shall have finished their testimony, the beast that ascendeth out of the bottomless pit shall make war against them, and shall overcome them, and kill them. And their dead bodies shall lie in the street of the great city, which spiritually is called Sodom and Egypt, where also our Lord was crucified. And they of the people and kindreds and tongues and nations shall see their dead bodies three days and an half, and shall not suffer their dead bodies to be put in graves. And they that dwell upon the earth shall rejoice over them, and make merry, and shall send gifts one to another; because these two prophets tormented them that dwelt on the earth. And after three days and an half the spirit of life from God entered into them, and they stood upon their feet; and great fear fell upon them which saw them. And they heard a great voice from heaven saying unto them, Come up hither. And they ascended up to heaven in a cloud; and their enemies beheld them. And the same hour was there a great earthquake,

> and the tenth part of the city fell,
> and in the earthquake were slain of
> men seven thousand: and the
> remnant were affrighted, and gave
> glory to the God of heaven
> (Revelation 11:7-13.)

At the end of the first 3½ year period, God will allow the Antichrist to kill the two witnesses. Their deaths can only come when their mission is over. Whether the Antichrist himself will murder them or what method will be used is unknown, but this will bring him world support and fame. Those on the earth will be so happy, worldwide celebrations will take place. Holiday's will be declared, and the Bible says, many around the world will literally exchange gifts in celebration of their deaths (Revelation 11:10). As a show of disrespect, the bodies of the witnesses will be on worldwide display in the streets of Jerusalem for 3½ days. They won't even get a decent burial.

At the end of the 3½ days, just as the party is warming up, God will cause the two witnesses to come back to life. This will stop the party cold. As the world looks on, a voice will call down from heaven and life will enter them. They will then stand to their feet and ascend up into heaven. This will strike terror into every corner of the world. Those who had terrorized the world, who were dead, are now alive again.

Before a red alert can be declared, Jerusalem is struck with a violent earthquake. The devastation levels a tenth of the city and claims 7,000 lives. Although, many will see this as a supernatural occurrence, they will not repent.

Activities Of The False Prophet And What Could Happen At The Midway Point Of The Tribulation Period

I will now introduce a seldom mentioned character who will play a significant role in the last world empire. He is the false prophet. It is not completely clear when the false prophet will come on the scene, but it is likely he will come on the world stage at the beginning of the tribulation period when the Antichrist is revealed. I suspect he will remain behind the scenes until the Antichrist demands world worship at the midway point of the tribulation.

It's not apparent what position he will hold but his mission is clear. I believe he will head up the world church. I am quite sure that he is alive and well today in the world church system although his future rise is not yet apparent to him. He will work his way up through the future global religious system and one day ascend to its highest position, but in the end, he will betray them. His power will be astonishing and his bond with the Antichrist will be unshakeable. From Dwight Pentecost's book *Things To Come* is a description of the false prophet and his purpose:

> In close association with the Beast, the head of the federated empire, is another individual known as the "False Prophet" (Rev. 19:20; 20: 10), called "the second beast" in Revelation 13:11-17, where his fullest description is given. In that passage of Scripture there are some important factors concerning him to be observed: (1) This individual is evidently a Jew, since he arises out of the earth, or land, that is Palestine (13: 11); (2) he is influential in religious affairs (13: 11, "two horns like a lamb"); (3) he is motivated by Satan as the first beast is (13:11); (4) he has a delegated authority (13:12, "the power of the first beast"); (5) he promotes the worship of the first beast and compels the earth to worship the first beast as God (13:12); (6) his ministry is authenticated by the signs and miracles which he does, evidently proving that he is Elijah that was to come (13:13-14); (7) he is successful in deceiving the unbelieving world (13:14); (8) the worship promoted is an idolatrous worship (13:14-15); (9) he has the power of death to compel men to worship the beast (13:15);

(10) he has authority in the economic realm to control all commerce (13:16-17); (11) he has a mark that will establish his identity for those who live in that day (13:18).[5]

Although the false prophet will eventually be as powerful as the Antichrist, his only goal will be to promote the worship of the beast. In further discussion about the false prophet, Charles C. Ryrie goes on to say in his book *Revelation* that, "in order to accomplish his aim, this second beast (false prophet) will be empowered to do certain things...He will make fire come down on the earth in imitation of the power of the two witnesses, to show the world that he has as much power as they had."[6]

He will act as a spokesperson for the Antichrist and erect a statue that he will cause to speak. This statue will command that every person on earth take a mark (666) either on the forehead or right hand (Revelation 13:13-18).

In doing these miracles, he will deceive the world into worshipping the Antichrist as God. God will allow this display of wizardry to ultimately sift out those who will serve Him from those who will serve the Antichrist.

---

[5] Pentecost, Dwight J. 1980. *Things To Come.* Grand Rapids, MI: Zondervan Publishing House, 336-37.

[6] Ryrie, Charles C. 1996. *Revelation, New Edition.* Chicago, IL: Moody Publishers, 98.

Around the midway point of the tribulation period, Satan will take possession of the Antichrist and proceed toward his ultimate plan. Of course, at this time, Satan has lost the war in heaven and has been confined to the earth (Revelation 12:7-9). It's unknown whether Satan will possess the Antichrist before or after he declares himself to be God, but in a surprise twist of events, someone assassinates the Antichrist. I'm sure this will send shock waves around the world. What happens next is described in Revelation 13:2-4:

> And the beast which I saw was like unto a leopard, and his feet were as the feet of a bear, and his mouth as the mouth of a lion: and the dragon gave him his power, and his seat, and great authority. And I saw one of his heads as it were wounded to death; and his deadly wound was healed: and all the world wondered after the beast. And they worshipped the dragon which gave power unto the beast: and they worshipped the beast, saying, Who is like unto the beast? who is able to make war with him?

As shocking as his assassination will be, somehow he will rise again. Just as Christ died and rose again, the Antichrist will duplicate this same feat. How he is healed or by what power is not apparent. We can only guess that

Satan is behind this false resurrection and God has allowed it to happen. This will complete the unholy death and resurrection of the Antichrist imitating the Holy Trinity of God. Satan corresponds to God the Father, the Antichrist corresponds to Jesus the Son, and the false prophet corresponds to the Holy Spirit. As God the Father gives all His power to Jesus, and the Holy Spirit does honor to Jesus, so Satan gives all his power to the Antichrist, and the false prophet gives honor to the Antichrist.

The world will be mesmerized by the Antichrist who was dead and now has come back to life. He will declare himself to be God and command that the entire world worship him and freely they will. With the false prophet at his side and Satan indwelling him, the world will see him as a messiah. For they will say, "Who is like the beast? Who is able to make war with him (Revelation 13:4b)?" He will literally trick the world into worshipping him.

Immediately, the Antichrist will break his treaty with the Jews and declare war and a mass execution. Although many will die, God will intervene and protect his people providing a hiding place that they may find refuge for the remaining 3½ years (Revelation 12:6).

Satan Indwells The Antichrist

As stated earlier, Satan and his army of demons are now confined to the earth. His first move will be to indwell the Antichrist and take control of the world through him.

After the defeat of the Russian-Islamic coalition, the Antichrist and the false prophet, at some point, will move their world headquarters from Rome to Jerusalem. After their great victory and salvation of Israel, I'm sure they will receive them with great celebration and honor. It is at this point that the Antichrist will make his bid for world dominance. But first, he must free himself from those who rule over him (Revelation 17:1-18).

Is Mystery Babylon Modern Day America?

> And there followed another angel, saying, Babylon is fallen, is fallen, that great city, because she made all nations drink of the wine of the wrath of her fornication.
>
> For all nations have drunk of the wine of the wrath of her fornication, and the kings of the earth have committed fornication with her, and the merchants of the earth are waxed rich through the abundance of her delicacies (Revelation 14:8; 18:3).

Much speculation has been raised over "Mystery Babylon". Is it a country, empire or system of some sort? Is it symbolic or literal? Is

Babylon religious, commercial or political? What does the Bible have to say about this mysterious Babylon?

During the tribulation period there will be a nation that will rule over the Antichrist and his ten nation kingdom (Revelation. 17:1-18). Not only will this country have great worldwide political power, it will also be very wealthy and religious in nature. Notice in the description that Babylon is pictured as a harlot riding a beast (Antichrist). The beast has ten horns (revived Roman Empire) representing ten nations which are subject to the beast. In essence, Mystery Babylon has given the beast and the ten nations their power, but remains very much in control. This will change toward the middle of the tribulation period.

Although many Bible scholars denounce this conclusion, I believe Mystery Babylon could be the United States. Many experts believe, in the years to come, the economic tide will turn toward the European Union and lead to the decline of America. When the Christian influence is taken out of America, hedonism and materialism will shift into high gear. Revelation 18:13 proclaims that they will sell anything for profit, "...cinnamon and incense, fragrant oil and frankincense, wine and oil, fine flour and wheat, cattle and sheep, horses and chariots, and bodies and souls of men."

Babylon is described more fully in Revelation 18 and has a striking resemblance to the United States. This chapter not only describes the demise of this country, but the magnitude of its world economic greatness. Following the complete destruction of Babylon, the Bible says, the kings of the earth and merchants of the sea wept and moaned over her desolation:

> And saying, Alas, alas that great city, that was clothed in fine linen, and purple, and scarlet, and decked with gold, and precious stones, and pearls! For in one hour so great riches is come to nought. And every shipmaster, and all the company in ships, and sailors, and as many as trade by sea, stood afar off, and cried when they saw the smoke of her burning, saying, What city is like unto this great city! And they cast dust on their heads, and cried, weeping and wailing, saying, Alas, alas that great city, wherein were made rich all that had ships in the sea by reason of her costliness! for in one hour is she made desolate (Revelation 18:16-19).

This is talking about a country that is considered the greatest commercial profit center of its time. No other nation can even be compared to its great wealth. All the nations of the world have become rich due to their trade with this country. The merchants of this nation were known as the great men of the world. When Babylon is destroyed world trade will be devastated. This will be a great worldwide loss both financially and politically.

Not only will Babylon be destroyed, its destruction will be swift and decisive, leading me to believe that this will be an all-out nuclear attack. It is my opinion that there will be few if any survivors. This is how the Bible describes its demise.

> And a mighty angel took up a stone like a great millstone, and cast it into the sea, saying, Thus with violence shall that great city Babylon be thrown down, and shall be found no more at all. And the voice of harpers, and musicians, and of pipers, and trumpeters, shall be heard no more at all in thee; and no craftsman, of whatsoever craft he be, shall be found any more in thee; and the sound of a millstone shall be heard no more at all in thee; And the light of a candle shall shine no more at all in thee; and the voice of the bridegroom and of the bride shall be heard no more at all in thee: for thy merchants were the great men of the earth; for by thy sorceries were all nations deceived. And in her was found the blood of prophets, and of saints,

and of all that were slain upon the earth (Revelation 18:21-24).

The destruction of this country will be so severe that it will be uninhabitable. Not even the light of one lamp will be found in this place. For in one day it will be reduced to rubble.

Whether Mystery Babylon is indeed the US is unknown, but given the description, it certainly does allude to that possibility. If this is the case, this war will probably take place just after Satan possesses the Antichrist toward the middle of the tribulation period. Satan will destroy this once great nation to rid himself of any challengers to his global throne.

The Religious Side of Mystery Babylon

The Bible says there will also be a religious side to Mystery Babylon. Although the religious headquarters will be located in Rome, the United States will have a strong voice as it does today.

Some believe, after the rapture occurs, many of the religions of the world will band together and form a one world religion to worship God. It will not be a Christ centered religion but a one God under many different names religion.

The World Council of Churches will probably place its headquarters at the Vatican and the Pope (possibly the false prophet) could lead it.

Although Rome will be the world headquarters, the United States will be its powerful ally.

God looks at this religious system as a harlot because it has become interwoven with the world. They have a form of God, but in reality, are no more than a religious order.

Religious Babylon is not a physical country with a standing army, but a literal system that will have worldwide influence in many powerful countries. Both the Antichrist and the religious system will use each other to gain position and power. But in the end, the false prophet, as a wolf in sheep's clothing, will betray Religious Babylon and promote the Antichrist as God. This betrayal will likely come around the midway point of the tribulation period when Mystery Babylon is destroyed and could happen as late as following the Antichrist's declaration that he is God.

Mystery Babylon Scenario

At this point we are about 3½ to 4 years into the tribulation period. This is the scenario I see for religious and political Babylon.

Let's speculate future political Babylon is the United States and the World Council of Churches is the religious side of the empire. Both will rule together as a wealthy, politically, and spiritually powerful partnership. The World Council of Churches will rule from Rome and the US will rule the world through the United Nations as it does today. At the beginning of the tribulation period, I believe the Antichrist will come on the world stage through the EU. For the first 3½ years the US (Babylon) will control the Antichrist and his 10 nation confederacy.

At around the middle of the tribulation period, Satan and his demons will be cast out of heaven permanently and confined to the earth. He will at this time enter the Antichrist. This will start the beginning of the end for the US and the World Council of Churches. For Satan would not be ruled over by God, and will not tolerate being ruled over by man. God, at this time, will use the Antichrist and his nations to exact judgment upon this wicked nation (Mystery Babylon).

> And the ten horns which thou sawest upon the beast, these shall hate the whore, and shall make her desolate and naked, and shall eat her flesh, and burn her with fire. For God hath put in their hearts to fulfil his will, and to agree, and give their kingdom unto the beast, until the words of God shall be fulfilled (Revelation 17:16-17).

The Antichrist and his ten nation confederacy will turn on the U.S., and what allies it may have, and launch an all-out nuclear attack.

The defeat is so swift and decisive it will leave the rest of the world terrified and shocked. For this was the greatest nation on the face of the earth and in one hour they have been completely destroyed! Kings, dignitaries, and businessmen are all left wondering what will happen next as they scramble to recoup losses and position themselves for what may happen with this dramatic change of power.

With the defeat of Israel's last ally, the Antichrist will march into the Jerusalem temple and stop the daily sacrifices. He will then desecrate the temple and declare himself to be God. Immediately, he will order that all other religions must cease and be disbanded, claiming that he is the only true god. Although the false prophet is the leader of the world religious system, he will betray them. His ultimate plan and only purpose from this day forward will be to promote the Antichrist as God (Revelation 13:11-17).

The Antichrist, along with the false prophet, will turn on the once proud religious system, destroy her buildings, set fire to her holy books, and kill her priests.

The Antichrist Sets Up His Throne

> Then I saw another beast coming up out of the earth, and he had two horns like a lamb and spoke like a dragon. And he exercises all the authority of the first beast in his

presence, and causes the earth and those who dwell in it to worship the first beast, whose deadly wound was healed. He performs great signs, so that he even makes fire come down from heaven on the earth in the sight of men. And he deceives those who dwell on the earth by those signs which he was granted to do in the sight of the beast, telling those who dwell on the earth to make an image to the beast who was wounded by the sword and lived. He was granted power to give breath to the image of the beast, that the image of the beast should both speak and cause as many as would not worship the image of the beast to be killed. He causes all, both small and great, rich and poor, free and slave, to receive a mark on their right hand or on their foreheads, and that no one may buy or sell except one who has the mark or the name of the beast, or the number of his name (Revelation 13:11-17).

Upon setting up his throne, the Antichrist will look to heaven and openly blaspheme God and the inhabitants of heaven. God will allow this to happen because He knows his (Antichrist) time will come.

The false prophet will officially begin promoting the Antichrist as God. In the presence of the Antichrist, he will perform great signs and wonders for the entire world to see. However, his greatest feat is still yet to come. The false prophet will command that an image of the Antichrist be created, and miraculously, he will bring the image to life and cause it to speak. I'm sure this will shock the world, but if that isn't enough, the image will command that everyone worldwide worship the Antichrist and take his mark (666).

He will then set up a world dictatorship and cause every man, woman and child, rich and poor, to take a mark either on the forehead or right hand. Everyone worldwide will take his mark and worship him except those who have accepted Jesus as Savior (Revelation 13:8). But before anyone takes the mark of the Antichrist, God will send angels to the earth to preach the Gospel and to warn them of the consequences of such a move.

> And I saw another angel fly in the midst of heaven, having the everlasting gospel to preach unto them that dwell on the earth, and to every nation, and kindred, and tongue, and people, Saying with a loud voice, Fear God, and give glory to him; for the hour of his judgment is come: and worship him that made heaven, and earth, and the sea, and

the fountains of waters. And there followed another angel, saying, Babylon is fallen, is fallen, that great city, because she made all nations drink of the wine of the wrath of her fornication. And the third angel followed them, saying with a loud voice, If any man worship the beast and his image, and receive his mark in his forehead, or in his hand, the same shall drink of the wine of the wrath of God, which is poured out without mixture into the cup of his indignation; and he shall be tormented with fire and brimstone in the presence of the holy angels, and in the presence of the Lamb: And the smoke of their torment ascendeth up for ever and ever: and they have no rest day nor night, who worship the beast and his image, and whosoever receiveth the mark of his name (Revelation 14:6-11).

Angels will literally be flying through the air proclaiming the Gospel of Jesus Christ understandable in every language on the planet. They will also carry a strong message for those who do decide to take the mark. Anyone who takes the mark or worships the Antichrist will be eternally damned to the lake of fire. This supernatural event will take place just after the halfway point of the tribulation period (3½ years).

It should also be noted, between the message of the first and third angel, the second angel announces that Mystery Babylon has fallen. This leads me to believe that this end-time dynasty will be destroyed just after the Antichrist declares himself to be God. It's very likely that many nations will not accept his announced plan for world dictatorship to well. This could be when the Antichrist puts down (subdues) three kings as prophesied in Daniel 7:24.

Friend, when you begin to see these things happen, it's time to head for the mountains (if you haven't already; Matthew 24:15-22), or wherever your safe haven is, and put your survival plan in motion. Because following this series of events, the Bible says, "For then shall [there] be great tribulation, such as was not since the beginning of the world to this time, no, nor ever shall be (Matthew 24:21)."

The Sixth Seal Is Broken

The sixth seal is now broken. We are now about 4 years into the tribulation period. The unholy trinity has now succeeded in deceiving the world into worshipping them unhindered as God. They may think they are in control but God still pulls all the strings. It is at this time that God will show His awesome power. I believe this seal will begin the most dreadful time in the history of mankind known as "The Great Day Of The Lord."

> And I beheld when he had opened the sixth seal, and, lo, there was a great earthquake; and the sun became black as sackcloth of hair, and the moon became as blood; and the stars of heaven fell unto the earth, even as a fig tree casteth her untimely figs, when she is shaken of a mighty wind. And the heaven departed as a scroll when it is rolled together; and every mountain and island were moved out of their places. And the kings of the earth, and the great men, and the rich men, and the chief captains, and the mighty men, and every bondman, and every free man, hid themselves in the dens and in the rocks of the mountains; and said to the mountains and rocks, Fall on us, and hide us from the face of him that sitteth on the throne, and from the wrath of the Lamb: For the great day of his wrath is come; and who shall be able to stand (Revelation 6:12-17)?"

Right in the middle of Satan's apparent victory, the sixth seal is opened. The purpose of this seal will be to strike terror into the heart of those on the earth. Immediately, a great earthquake erupts. The earthquake is so devastating that it is felt worldwide. Every mountain and island will be moved. At the same time, I believe volcanoes from all over the world will explode, spewing volcanic ash miles into the air. The sun will turn black and the moon red. The stars of heaven will fall to the earth. Men both rich and poor, free and slave, will hide themselves for fear of the Lord.

Judging from the scriptures, the world apparently will view this great destruction as coming from the Lord. No one will mistake this great devastation as a simple natural disaster. But even in fear, the hardness of their hearts will not allow them to repent.

The Seventh Seal Is Broken

> And when he had opened the seventh seal, there was silence in heaven about the space of half an hour (Revelation 8:1).

After the massive worldwide earthquake, God calls for silence for about half an hour. The purpose of this silence will be to see what the reaction of man will be, whether they will continue to rebel or repent.

Some describe it as the calm before the storm. I believe this will be the last chance for man to obtain mercy. For at the end of the silence come the remaining judgments. These judgments will be so devastating and so horrible that Jesus said, "...And except those days should be shortened, there should no flesh be saved: but for the elect's sake those days shall be shortened (Matthew 24:22)."

The judgments will be released in order and consecutive one right after the other. First will be the 7 trumpet judgments (Revelation 8:7-9:21; Revelation 11:15-19) followed by 7 bowl judgments (Revelation 16:1-21).

Some consider these judgments to be the wrath of God, and therefore, believe Christians will be protected. "For God hath not appointed us to wrath, but to obtain salvation by our Lord Jesus Christ (I Thessalonians 5:9)."

That could be true, however, from the remaining judgments, only the fifth trumpet, first and fifth bowls are said to be specifically released upon the kingdom of the Antichrist (those who have taken the mark) or those who do not have the seal of God upon their forehead. I would only count on protection where the Bible specifically states Christians will be protected.

The First Trumpet Sounds

The first angel sounded, and there followed hail and fire mingled with blood, and they were cast upon the earth: and the third part of trees was burnt up, and all green grass was burnt up (Revelation 8:7).

We are now about 4½ to 5 years into the tribulation period when the first trumpet judgment sounds. Some Bible scholars believe that this represents an all-out nuclear war where God will leave man to destroy himself. I do not agree! The destruction is much too precise. This trumpet judgment will come directly from God. I believe that God will literally bring about a worldwide hailstorm. This hailstorm will be unlike any that man has ever encountered. These will be hailstones of fire and will bombard the earth unmercifully destroying one third of the trees and cover the ground like freshly fallen snow burning up all the grass.

I suspect, along with the loss of green grass will come a massive crop failure resulting in a mammoth food shortage. This will result in many wild animals, livestock, and people dying from starvation.

Trees act as a giant air filter for the world, continuously cleaning and re-cleaning the air. With one third less trees the air will barely be consumable. You will need to take this into consideration when preparing in advance for your survival needs.

An excellent gas mask is the Israeli military model M15. It has a drinking tube and an improved speaking port. The M15 protects against nuclear, biological, and chemical agents, and comes with a sealed filter holder. You can find this mask at many online military surplus stores. Again, do your research and select the most up-to-date mask available.

The Second Trumpet Sounds

> And the second angel sounded, and as it were a great mountain burning with fire was cast into the sea: and the third part of the sea became blood; and the third part of the creatures which were in the sea, and had life, died; and the third part of the ships were destroyed (Revelation 8:8-9).

The second trumpet judgment sounds. I will guess this judgment will take place within 1 to 3 months after the first trumpet judgment sounds. Notice again the preciseness of this judgment. One third of the sea became blood, causing one third of the sea life to die, and one third of the ships were destroyed. It is possible that war on the sea could breakout drawing many war ships to a proposed area, causing one third of the ships and sea life to perish. However, I think it is more likely that this judgment will come directly from the hand of God. Like the first trumpet, it will serve notice that though man has turned to the Antichrist, he is helpless to save them from the wrath to come.

It's not clear what this burning mountain is, but I believe John is describing an asteroid. Not just any asteroid, but one that is so enormous, upon impact it will melt, destroy, and disintegrate anything in its path.

Imagine if you will, a giant fireball the size of a country crashing into the ocean at a speed of 35 thousand miles per hour. Forget about the heat and the death of the sea creatures, the tidal wave that this impact will cause will be of epic proportions. The way I see it, any ships that are not immediately disintegrated from the intense heat will be destroyed by the giant tidal waves that follow. Needless to say, many people will die. It is advisable to stay away from coastal areas, especially where there may be a considerable concentration of ships.

The Third Trumpet Sounds

And the third angel sounded, and there fell a great star from heaven, burning as it were a lamp, and it fell upon the third part of the rivers, and upon the fountains of waters; and the name of the star is called Wormwood: and the third part of the waters became wormwood; and many men died of the waters,

because they were made bitter
(Revelation 8:10-11).

The third trumpet judgment sounds. God continues to systematically destroy the available natural resources so critical to man's existence. As He destroyed one third of the oceans and its creatures, now He will destroy one third of the rivers and springs. This will be a fatal blow considering one third of the available drinking water will be contaminated. Although the death toll is unknown, the Bible states that many men will die from drinking this water.

There is no way of knowing if the latest portable water purifying systems will be able to clean water contaminated by the star Wormwood. There is a toxic variety of the wormwood plant, but whether it is the same mentioned in this Scripture passage is unknown. Certainly, it will be necessary to boil all water following this trumpet judgment. It is advisable to make this a practice from day one of the tribulation period.

The Fourth Trumpet Sounds

And the fourth angel sounded, and the third part of the sun was smitten, and the third part of the moon, and the third part of the stars; so as the third part of them was darkened, and the day shone not for a third part of it, and the night likewise. And I beheld, and heard an angel flying through the midst of heaven, saying with a loud voice, Woe, woe, woe, to the inhabiters of the earth by reason of the other voices of the trumpet of the three angels, which are yet to sound (Revelation 8:12-13)!

The fourth trumpet judgment sounds. At this point, God now strikes the three natural sources of light by one third. Again, some scholars incorrectly try to link this with a nuclear holocaust. If this were caused by nuclear war, the dark skies would continue around the clock like a black haze. God, who is in precise control, simply turns out the lights so that a day is shorten by one third. I believe, that from this day forward, a day will only be 16 hours long. This would be consistent with what Jesus stated in Matthew 24:22, "And except those days should be shortened, there should no flesh be saved: but for the elect's sake those days shall be shortened." I do, however, believe the effects of the first trumpet judgment combined with nuclear war will present a lingering hazy sky.

Immediately, John looked up and saw an angel flying through heaven announcing that there are still 3 trumpets to be sounded. As horrible as the first four trumpets were, these last three will be even worse. So bad, the warning is emphasized with three "woes".

The Fifth Trumpet Sounds

And the fifth angel sounded, and I saw a star fall from heaven unto the earth: and to him was given the key of the bottomless pit. And he opened the bottomless pit; and there arose a smoke out of the pit, as the smoke of a great furnace; and the sun and the air were darkened by reason of the smoke of the pit. And there came out of the smoke locusts upon the earth: and unto them was given power, as the scorpions of the earth have power. And it was commanded them that they should not hurt the grass of the earth, neither any green thing, neither any tree; but only those men which have not the seal of God in their foreheads. And to them it was given that they should not kill them, but that they should be tormented five months: and their torment was as the torment of a scorpion, when he striketh a man. And in those days shall men seek death, and shall not find it; and shall desire to die, and death shall flee from them. And the shapes of the locusts were like unto horses prepared unto battle; and on their heads were as it were crowns like gold, and their faces were as the faces of men. And they had hair as the hair of women, and their teeth were as the teeth of lions. And they had breastplates, as it were breastplates of iron; and the sound of their wings was as the sound of chariots of many horses running to battle. And they had tails like unto scorpions, and there were stings in their tails: and their power was to hurt men five months. And they had a king over them, which is the angel of the bottomless pit, whose name in the Hebrew tongue is Abaddon, but in the Greek tongue hath his name Apollyon (Revelation 9:1-11).

The fifth trumpet, first woe sounds. At this time, we are about 5 to 5½ years into the tribulation period. This trumpet judgment begins a torment that one can only attempt to imagine. These creatures are literal beings that will be released for this specific time of tribulation. They are released by an angel. Some believe this angel to be Christ because He alone has the keys to death and hell (Revelation 1:18). Others believe it is Satan. Whoever this person is, he is given the authority to unlock the earthly opening into the pits of hell. Immediately, this unleashes the most horrible creatures ever created by God, and they are eager to engage in their mission. Their mission is simple: Do not harm the trees and vegetation nor kill any man, but torment those who do not have the seal of God. For five months, they will roam the earth seeking whom they might torment. The worst part about this situation, they won't be able to be destroyed. With all the hi-tech smart weaponry available nothing will stand in their way. The following scenario will give you a closer look into a nightmare I hope and pray you will not have to face.

Imagine, if you will, you're walking through what used to be a thickly wooded forest devastated by the fiery hailstorm. At a glance, it looks like the ravishes of a wildfire that has come and gone, feeding on anything and everything in its path.

These are dangerous times and particularly dangerous to those who journey alone. As you cautiously proceed down the ever deepening dark path, you can't help but wonder what awaits you. With every passing day the world seems to be plunging deeper and deeper into a dark age unimaginable by mankind. It's 2 PM and the sun is already beginning to set. You know you must find shelter soon or risk falling prey to wild animals.

Suddenly, the earth begins to shake violently. Thinking it's the beginning of another earthquake, you dive behind a nearby fallen tree. Securely behind the great oak, you brace for the worst. As the rumbling draws closer and closer, it becomes evident that this is not an earthquake. It sounds more like a stampede and it's heading your way. As you peer out from behind your hiding place, you can't believe your eyes. Thousands, maybe millions of horse-like creatures are flying through the air. It looked like something straight out of hell! It was unlike anything you'd ever seen.

Curious to see what these creatures were, you position yourself to get a better look. As strange as it may sound, they looked to have the face of a man with long flowing hair and a horse-like body with giant protruding wings resembling that of a bat. At the other end, appeared to be what looked like a tail. However, this was no ordinary tail. It coiled and uncoiled like a scorpion's tail as if it were waiting to strike. Their overall appearance was ferocious like some wild beast and they moved with stealth like precision.

Terrified that you might be noticed, you quickly move back as they pass overhead. But it's too late! You've been spotted by one of these devilish creatures. Thinking that your only chance is to flee, you begin to run with all your might toward a nearby patch of trees. If you can only make it into the forest you'll be safe. As you near the forest you can hear the sound of the creature's wings getting closer and closer. Your mind is racing a mile a minute like prey who has strayed from the pack...only thirty more feet...only twenty more feet. Your heart is pounding with every step as you grasp for what little hope may remain. However, to no avail, the creature has overtaken you knocking you to the ground. As you look up into his fiery eyes, you brace for the worst. As the creature stares intently down at you with his scorpion-like tail poised, he suddenly raises his head back and lets out a great roar revealing his razor-sharp teeth. Then to your amazement, he turns and flies away. As you slowly stand to your feet, you can't help but wonder why your life has been spared.

As the days go on, you will hear of many who will not be as fortunate. You will learn of the terror and pain inflicted by these creatures who have but one mission and purpose, to torment those of the earth who have not the seal of God. For in their tails lie the sting of a scorpion and the power to hurt men for five months. So awful will this torment be that men will seek to die, but God will not permit death to come.

The Sixth Trumpet Sounds

And the sixth angel sounded, and I heard a voice from the four horns of the golden altar which is before God, Saying to the sixth angel which had the trumpet, Loose the four angels which are bound in the great river Euphrates. And the four angels were loosed, which were prepared for an hour, and a day, and a month, and a year, for to slay the third part of men. And the number of the army of the horsemen were two hundred thousand thousand: and I heard the number of them. And thus I saw the horses in the vision, and them that sat on them, having breastplates of fire, and of jacinth, and brimstone: and the heads of the horses were as the heads of lions; and out of their mouths issued fire and smoke and brimstone. By these three was the third part of men killed, by the fire, and by the smoke, and by the brimstone, which issued out of their mouths. For their power is in their mouth, and in their tails: for their tails were like unto serpents, and had heads, and with them they do hurt (Revelation 9:13-19).

The sixth trumpet, second woe sounds. I would estimate that up to this point between 3-4 billion people have died. With the blast of the sixth trumpet will come the death of another one-third of the remaining world population. God will call for the release of the four demonic angels who have been prepared for this very moment to sweep from the East to the West. The size of this army will number 200 million. No one will be able to stop their military advancement. This will begin 13 months of death and destruction that will eventually climax at the Battle of Armageddon.

118

Who are these demonic leaders? Are they literal or symbolic demons? I believe these demons are literal military leaders who are set aside by God for this very day. It's unknown if the army will be demon possessed as well, however, more than a few Bible scholars believe they will be.

I would estimate we are heading into the final year of the tribulation period.

The Seventh Trumpet Sounds Releasing The Bowl Judgments

> And the seventh angel sounded; and there were great voices in heaven, saying, The kingdoms of this world are become the kingdoms of our Lord, and of his Christ; and he shall reign for ever and ever. And the four and twenty elders, which sat before God on their seats, fell upon their faces, and worshipped God, Saying, We give thee thanks, O Lord God Almighty, which art, and wast, and art to come; because thou hast taken to thee thy great power, and hast reigned. And the nations were angry, and thy wrath is come, and the time of the dead, that they should be judged, and that thou shouldest give reward unto thy servants the prophets, and to the saints, and them that fear thy name, small and great; and shouldest

destroy them which destroy the earth. And the temple of God was opened in heaven, and there was seen in his temple the ark of his testament: and there were lightnings, and voices, and thunderings, and an earthquake, and great hail.

And after that I looked, and, behold, the temple of the tabernacle of the testimony in heaven was opened: And the seven angels came out of the temple, having the seven plagues, clothed in pure and white linen, and having their breasts girded with golden girdles. And one of the four beasts gave unto the seven angels seven golden vials full of the wrath of God, who liveth for ever and ever. And the temple was filled with smoke from the glory of God, and from his power; and no man was able to enter into the temple, till the seven plagues of the seven angels were fulfilled. And I heard a great voice out of the temple saying to the seven angels, Go your ways, and pour out the vials of the wrath of God upon the earth (Revelation 11:15-19; 15:5-16:1).

All of heaven begins to rejoice because they know it is getting very close to the end. This group of judgments will likely take place toward the end of the seventh and final year of the tribulation period.

This time, all 7 angels are each given a bowl (vial judgment) and instructed to immediately go and pour it out onto the earth. Most experts believe they will be poured out one right after the other without delay. It will be like a firework's grand finale.

The First Bowl Judgment

> And the first went, and poured out his vial upon the earth; and there fell a noisome and grievous sore upon the men which had the mark of the beast, and upon them which worshipped his image (Revelation 16:2).

The first bowl judgment was cast out onto the earth, and great and repulsive smelling boils broke out on everyone who had taken the mark and worshiped the Antichrist. These boils will not only be big and smelly they will be very painful. They might even be cancerous.

The Second Bowl Judgment

> And the second angel poured out his vial upon the sea; and it became as the blood of a dead man: and

every living soul died in the sea
(Revelation 16:3).

The second angel poured out his bowl upon the
oceans turning them to blood and killing every
creature. From this day forward all oceans will
stink with the smell of death.

The Third Bowl Judgment

> And the third angel poured out his
> vial upon the rivers and fountains
> of waters; and they became blood
> (Revelation 16:4).

The third angel pours out his bowl upon the
rivers and springs, and they too are turned to
blood. Now all fresh drinking water is completely
polluted and every living creature therein is
killed.

Systematically, God is eliminating what is left
of all available natural resources. Without
drinking water, it will only be a matter of days
before the entire world population will simply
die due to consumption or dehydration.

Later, the angel of the waters proclaims that
the Lord's judgments are righteous and true.
For they have shed the blood of the Saints and
of the prophets, and now they are repaid with
blood to drink.

Given the proclamation by the angel, most Bible
prophecy scholars believe all fresh water

sources will be turned to blood but will not be toxic. This is the time the Katadyn Pocket Water Micofilter and the SteriPEN Traveler Handheld Water Purifier (or whatever the latest purifying technology is) will be of great value. Blood by volume is about 50% water. Using these two portable water purifying systems in concert should filter out all impurities and provide safe and clean water even from pure blood.

I would estimate we are only weeks to a few months away from the end of the tribulation period.

The Fourth Bowl Judgment

> And the fourth angel poured out his vial upon the sun; and power was given unto him to scorch men with fire. And men were scorched with great heat, and blasphemed the name of God, which hath power over these plagues: and they repented not to give him glory (Revelation 16:8-9).

Imagine that all the known resources of drinking water have been polluted rendering them unfit for human consumption. Next, the Lord sends a great heat so severe that it scorches everyone that is exposed to its rays.

Some prophecy experts believe the heat will be so intense that it will cause the great ice caps of Antarctica and surrounding areas to melt resulting in major flooding worldwide. I would assume that the lack of clean drinking water compounded by great heat would only accelerate the death toll.

The Fifth Bowl Judgment

> And the fifth angel poured out his vial upon the seat of the beast; and his kingdom was full of darkness; and they gnawed their tongues for pain, and blasphemed the God of heaven because of their pains and their sores, and repented not of their deeds (Revelation 16:10-11).

The fifth angel pours out his bowl, and a great darkness covers the kingdom of the Antichrist, including his ten nation kingdom. It is stated that "they gnawed their tongues because of the pain". It's not apparent what part of this fifth bowl judgment has caused this pain. It is likely that God has intensified their sores from the first bowl judgment.

Despite knowing this to be the judgment of God, they not only refuse to repent, but compound it by openly blaspheming God.

The Sixth Bowl Judgment

> And the sixth angel poured out his vial upon the great river Euphrates;

> and the water thereof was dried up,
> that the way of the kings of the east
> might be prepared. And I saw three
> unclean spirits like frogs come out
> of the mouth of the dragon, and out
> of the mouth of the beast, and out
> of the mouth of the false prophet.
> For they are the spirits of devils,
> working miracles, which go forth
> unto the kings of the earth and of
> the whole world, to gather them to
> the battle of that great day of God
> Almighty. Behold, I come as a thief.
> Blessed is he that watcheth, and
> keepeth his garments, lest he walk
> naked, and they see his shame. And
> he gathered them together into a
> place called in the Hebrew tongue
> Armageddon (Revelation 16:12-16).

This, of course, will be the gathering of all the great nations of the earth for the final battle at Armageddon. God will cause the Euphrates River to be dried up to expedite this operation. The unholy trinity will deceive the nations into joining in league with them to once and for all destroy Israel.

This battle between Satan and God will climax at the Valley of Megiddo, better known as Armageddon (Har Megiddo).

The Seventh Bowl Judgment

> And the seventh angel poured out his vial into the air; and there came a great voice out of the temple of heaven, from the throne, saying, It is done. And there were voices, and thunders, and lightnings; and there was a great earthquake, such as was not since men were upon the earth, so mighty an earthquake, and so great. And the great city was divided into three parts, and the cities of the nations fell: and great Babylon came in remembrance before God, to give unto her the cup of the wine of the fierceness of his wrath. And every island fled away, and the mountains were not found. And there fell upon men a great hail out of heaven, every stone about the weight of a talent: and men blasphemed God because of the plague of the hail; for the plague thereof was exceeding great (Revelation 16:17-21).

When the seventh bowl judgment is poured out, a loud voice proclaims "it is done". At this point, the tribulation period is coming to a close, and it could be only a few hours away before Jesus descends for His second coming.

126

However, before He descends, the most powerful worldwide earthquake in the history of mankind strikes. The Bible says it will be so devastating, it will flatten every city and mountain on the face of the earth, and every island will suddenly disappear. The fallen city of Babylon, the great financial center previously destroyed, will be split into three parts. If that isn't enough, a great global hailstorm will rain down 100 lbs. hailstones upon man. I'm sure the death toll will be staggering.

Earlier in this book, I shared a verse of Scripture where Jesus said, "When ye therefore shall see the abomination of desolation, spoken of by Daniel the prophet, stand in the holy place, (whoso readeth, let him understand:) Then let them which be in Judaea flee into the mountains (Matthew 24:15-16)".

Now we are coming to the end of the tribulation period, and the Lord has completely flattened all cities and mountains around the world. He has also submerged every island. If you have taken up refuge in a mountainous hideaway or on a deserted island, according to Scripture, it would be highly advisable to descend from the mountain and to get off that island. I would certainly be aware of the signs leading up to this bowl judgment to avoid being a casualty.

Part 4:
Second Coming Of Christ, Judgment Of Nations & Salvation

The Second Coming Of Christ

And I saw heaven opened, and behold a white horse; and he that sat upon him was called Faithful and True, and in righteousness he doth judge and make war. His eyes were as a flame of fire, and on his head were many crowns; and he had a name written, that no man knew, but he himself. And he was clothed with a vesture dipped in blood: and his name is called The Word of God. And the armies which were in heaven followed him upon white horses, clothed in fine linen, white and clean. And out of his mouth goeth a sharp sword, that with it he should smite the nations: and he shall rule them with a rod of iron: and he treadeth the winepress of the fierceness and wrath of Almighty God. And he hath on his vesture and on his thigh a name written, KING OF KINGS, AND LORD OF LORDS. And I saw an angel standing in the sun; and he cried with a loud voice, saying to all the fowls that fly in the midst of heaven, Come and gather yourselves together unto the supper of the great God; That ye may eat the flesh of kings, and the flesh of captains, and the flesh of mighty men, and the flesh of horses, and of them that sit on them, and the flesh of all men, both free and bond, both small and great. And I saw the beast, and the kings of the earth, and their armies, gathered together to make war against him that sat on the horse, and against his army (Revelation 19:11-19).

At this time, the Lord will gather the nations of the earth together for His final triumph. The Lord's army will be comprised of resurrected New Testament Saints and a great host of angels. The human army will embody those who have pledged their allegiance to the Antichrist and have taken his mark. Both rich and poor, bond and free, great and small will participate in this battle, however, it will be over before it starts.

As the Lord descends from heaven, He will split the eastern skies (Matthew 24:27) and physically touch down on the Mount of Olives. This will cause the mount to literally divide down the middle and a great earthquake will follow (Zechariah 14:4-5).

Behold, the day of the LORD cometh, and thy spoil shall be divided in the midst of thee. For I will gather all nations against

Jerusalem to battle; and the city shall be taken, and the houses rifled, and the women ravished; and half of the city shall go forth into captivity, and the residue of the people shall not be cut off from the city. Then shall the LORD go forth, and fight against those nations, as when he fought in the day of battle (Zechariah 14:1-3).

The Bible says, at the sound of the Lord's voice, their bodies will rot where they stand (Zechariah 14:12). In fact, it is described as a great winepress in which Christ literally crushes His foes and their blood will flow approximately 4 feet high and 200 miles long. The slaughter will be so great that God will call the birds of the air to come and gorge themselves on the flesh of men (Revelation 19:11-19).

This will be a supernatural event that the Bible says every eye will see. The world will mourn (Matthew 24:30) as they see Jesus returning in the sky while tribulation Christians will rejoice. This will mean the doom of all those who have taken the mark and worshiped the Antichrist. They will be captured and cast into the lake of fire (Revelation 14:9-11). Tribulation Christians, on the other hand, will enter into the millennial Reign of Christ where they will enjoy unprecedented blessing in a near-perfect environment for 1,000 years. I say near-perfect because, although Jesus will rule, He will have to rule the nations with a rod of iron (Revelation 19:15).

The Capture Of The Unholy Trinity

> And the beast was taken, and with him the false prophet that wrought miracles before him, with which he deceived them that had received the mark of the beast, and them that worshipped his image. These both were cast alive into a lake of fire burning with brimstone. And the remnant were slain with the sword of him that sat upon the horse, which sword proceeded out of his mouth: and all the fowls were filled with their flesh. And I saw an angel come down from heaven, having the key of the bottomless pit and a great chain in his hand. And he laid hold on the dragon, that old serpent, which is the Devil, and Satan, and bound him a thousand years, and cast him into the bottomless pit, and shut him up, and set a seal upon him, that he should deceive the nations no more, till the thousand years should be fulfilled: and after that he must be loosed a little season (Revelation 19:20-20:3).

Following the Lord's miraculous and stunning victory at Armageddon (Fig. 3), the Antichrist and the false prophet will be hunted down and cast into the lake of fire where they will be tormented forever and ever. Satan will then be captured, bound for 1,000 years, and thrown into the bottomless pit.

There will be 75 days (Daniel 12:11-13) between the second coming and the beginning of the millennial Reign of Christ. The first thing Jesus will do is

FIGURE 3: LOCATION OF ARMAGEDDON

judge the nations. It should be stated that the word "nations" should not be taken as whole countries, but individuals. Although, in some cases, whole nations may be wiped out and cast into the lake of fire.

This judgment of the nations is described in Matthew 25:31-46. First to be judged are those who survived the tribulation period but took the mark and worshiped the Antichrist. They will immediately be cast alive into the lake of fire for an eternity (Revelation 19:20).

Those who did not take the mark of the Antichrist nor worship his image, but accepted the Lord Jesus as Savior will be spared. They will be granted access to enter into the Millennium where most will enjoy a long life on earth for the entire 1,000 year reign of Christ (Isaiah 65:19-23). For those who are granted entrance, as horrible as the tribulation period was, those days will be forgotten against the great blessings and prosperity of the millennial Reign of Christ. Jesus will reign supreme and "in that day shall there be upon the bells of the horses, HOLINESS UNTO THE LORD (Zechariah 14:20a)".

This day is coming, but before it arrives, the rapture will take place plunging the world into great tribulation. Will you be left behind? Have you already been left behind? Worst yet, will you be one of the individuals who will take the mark and worship the Antichrist, and ultimately be cast into the lake of fire for an eternity? Do you know the Lord? If you cannot positively affirm that you know Him, please keep reading!

How To Be Saved

When Jesus does rapture the church, billions of people will be left behind to face the most horrifying time in world history. But there is a place that's worse than the horrors of the tribulation period and it's an eternal hell. Trust me, you don't want to chance ending up in this awful place. For it is a place of burning, weeping, and agonizing pain that will never end throughout all eternity (Luke 16:19-31).

You may say, I certainly don't want to end up there. How can I escape hell and gain eternal life in heaven? There's only one way and it's through the death, burial, and resurrection of Jesus Christ. It is only through His finished work on the cross that you and I can be saved (go to heaven). You can't get there through your various good works or because you are a good person. If we were good enough, then Jesus wasted His time dying for our sins.

Please take the time to ask yourself this question. Do you positively know you have a personal relationship with Jesus? If this is a big question mark in your life don't take a chance. The only way to know for sure is to ask Jesus to take control of your life, repent of your sins, place Him first in your life, and never look back. Only Jesus can save you and present you spotless until that final day.

If you would like to accept Jesus as Lord please pray with me right now:

Father, I know that I am a sinner and cannot obtain salvation in and of myself. I come to You in the name of Jesus asking that You forgive me of my sins, and to cleanse me from all unrighteousness and guilt. I trust and believe that Jesus died and rose again to pay my sin penalty. I accept Your free gift of salvation, and from this day forward, turn my life completely over to You Lord. I thank You and praise You God for giving me a new life in Christ. Amen.

If you have prayed this prayer and committed your life to Jesus you are now a Christian. However, there will likely come a time when you will be tortured and/or killed for your faith in Jesus Christ. It is important that you stay strong in the Lord and in the power of His might (Ephesians 6:10). Don't allow anyone or anything to deceive you into denying the Lord. And above all, don't take the mark of the Antichrist or worship him...even if it means death (Revelation 13)! If you do, know that your eternal future will be to be cast into the lake of fire forever (Revelation 14:9-11).

May the Lord be with you and keep you in these last days as you await His return in the clouds of Glory.

Part 5:
Tribulation Period Charts & Other Survival Resources

Tribulation Period
1st Half

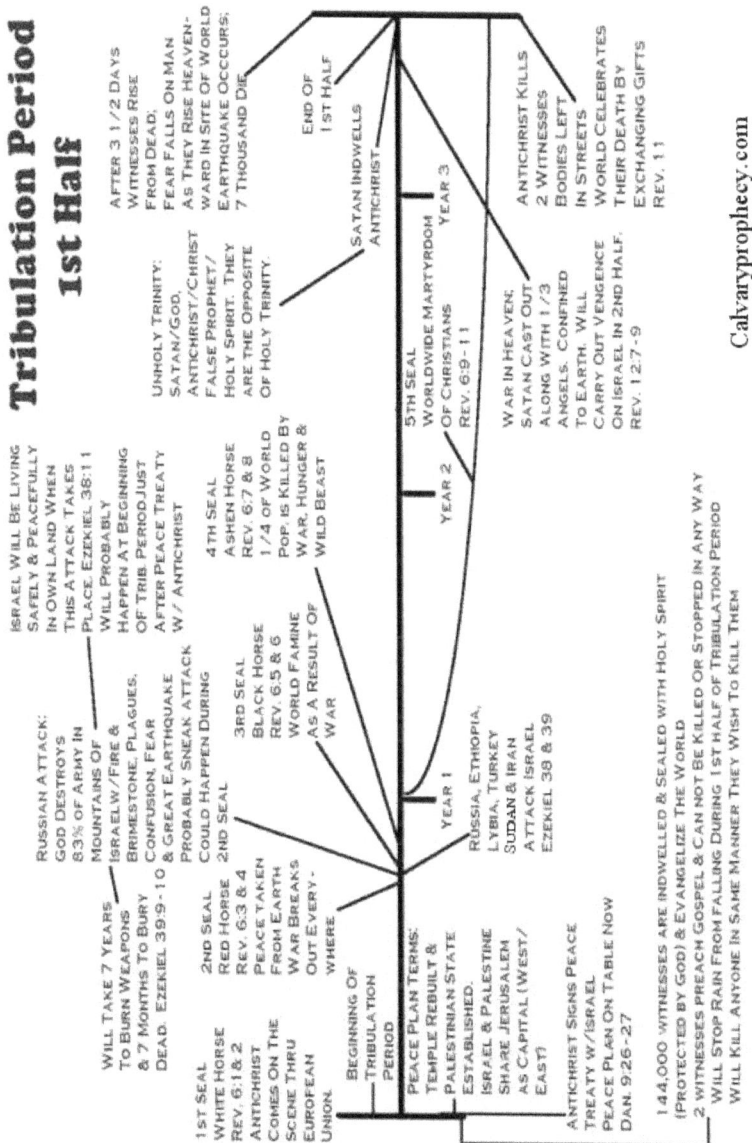

RUSSIAN ATTACK:
GOD DESTROYS
83% OF ARMY IN
MOUNTAINS OF
ISRAEL W/FIRE &
BRIMESTONE, PLAGUES,
CONFUSION, FEAR
& GREAT EARTHQUAKE
DEAD. EZEKIEL 39:9-10

WILL TAKE 7 YEARS
TO BURN WEAPONS
& 7 MONTHS TO BURY

ISRAEL WILL BE LIVING
SAFELY & PEACEFULLY
IN OWN LAND WHEN
THIS ATTACK TAKES
PLACE. EZEKIEL 38:11
WILL PROBABLY
HAPPEN AT BEGINNING
OF TRIB PERIOD JUST
AFTER PEACE TREATY
W/ ANTICHRIST

AFTER 3 1/2 DAYS
WITNESSES RISE
FROM DEAD;
FEAR FALLS ON MAN
AS THEY RISE HEAVEN-
WARD IN SITE OF WORLD
EARTHQUAKE OCCURS;
7 THOUSAND DIE

UNHOLY TRINITY:
SATAN/GOD,
ANTICHRIST/CHRIST
FALSE PROPHET/
HOLY SPIRIT. THEY
ARE THE OPPOSITE
OF HOLY TRINITY.

1ST SEAL
WHITE HORSE
REV. 6:1 & 2
ANTICHRIST
COMES ON THE
SCENE THRU
EUROPEAN
UNION.

2ND SEAL
RED HORSE
REV. 6:3 & 4
PEACE TAKEN
FROM EARTH
WAR BREAKS
OUT EVERY-
WHERE.

PROBABLY SNEAK ATTACK
COULD HAPPEN DURING

3RD SEAL
BLACK HORSE
REV. 6:5 & 6
WORLD FAMINE
AS A RESULT OF
WAR

4TH SEAL
ASHEN HORSE
REV. 6:7 & 8
1/4 OF WORLD
POP. IS KILLED BY
WAR, HUNGER &
WILD BEAST

END OF
1ST HALF

SATAN INDWELLS
ANTICHRIST

BEGINNING OF
TRIBULATION
PERIOD

PEACE PLAN TERMS:
TEMPLE REBUILT &
PALESTINIAN STATE
ESTABLISHED.
ISRAEL & PALESTINE
SHARE JERUSALEM
AS CAPITAL (WEST/
EAST)

YEAR 1

RUSSIA, ETHIOPIA,
LYBIA, TURKEY
SUDAN & IRAN
ATTACK ISRAEL
EZEKIEL 38 & 39

YEAR 2

5TH SEAL
WORLDWIDE MARTYRDOM
OF CHRISTIANS
REV. 6:9-11

YEAR 3

ANTICHRIST KILLS
2 WITNESSES
BODIES LEFT
IN STREETS
WORLD CELEBRATES
THEIR DEATH BY
EXCHANGING GIFTS
REV. 11

WAR IN HEAVEN:
SATAN CAST OUT
ALONG WITH 1/3
ANGELS. CONFINED
TO EARTH. WILL
CARRY OUT VENGENCE
ON ISRAEL IN 2ND HALF.
REV. 12:7-9

ANTICHRIST SIGNS PEACE
TREATY W/ISRAEL
PEACE PLAN ON TABLE NOW
DAN. 9:26-27

144,000 WITNESSES ARE INDWELLED & SEALED WITH HOLY SPIRIT
(PROTECTED BY GOD) & EVANGELIZE THE WORLD
2 WITNESSES PREACH GOSPEL & CAN NOT BE KILLED OR STOPPED IN ANY WAY
WILL STOP RAIN FROM FALLING DURING 1ST HALF OF TRIBULATION PERIOD
WILL KILL ANYONE IN SAME MANNER THEY WISH TO KILL THEM

Calvaryprophecy.com

Tribulation Period 2nd Half

AFTER SILENCE (7TH SEAL) ANGELS FLY THRU AIR WARNING NOT TO TAKE MARK. AT THIS POINT NO ONE HAS TAKEN MARK REV. 14:6-11

MYSTERY BABYLON LORDED POWER OVER ANTICHRIST WILL BE DESTROYED BY TEN-KINGDOM EMPIRE OF ANTICHRIST REV. 17:1-18

ANTICHRIST DESTROYS MYSTERY BABYLON & FALSE PROPHET BETRAYS WORLD CHURCH

6TH & 7TH SEAL GREAT WORLDWIDE EARTHQUAKE WORLDWIDE FEAR SILENCE IN HEAVEN FOR 1/2 HOUR REV. 6:12-17; 8:1

3RD TRUMPET 1/3 OF RIVERS & STREAMS POISONED. (WORMWOOD) MANY DIE. REV. 8:10, 11

5TH BOWL DARKNESS FALLS UPON ANTICHRIST KINGDOM. BOILS PLAGUE REV. 16:10, 11

RETURN OF CHRIST W/ SAINTS MATT. 24

6TH BOWL EUPHRATES RIVER DRIES UP. AIDS IN ARMIES MARCH TO ARMAGEDDON REV. 16:12-16

4TH BOWL SUN SCORCHES MEN REV. 16:8-9

3RD BOWL RIVERS & FOUNTAINS BECOME BLOOD REV. 16:4

2ND BOWL SEA TURNED TO BLOOD ALL FISH DIE REV. 16:3

1ST BOWL BOILS BREAK OUT ON THOSE WHO HAVE TAKEN THE MARK REV. 16:2

BATTLE OF ARMAGEDDON NO SURVIVORS REV. 19:11-21

SATAN BOUND 1000 YEARS ANTICHRIST & FALSE PROPHET CAST IN LAKE OF FIRE. REV. 19:20-21; 20:1-3

6TH TRUMPET ARMY FROM EAST MARCHES TO WEST 200 MILLION STRONG MARCH WILL END AT ARMAGEDDON 1/3 WORLD POP KILLED REV. 9:13-19

4TH TRUMPET DAY SHORTENED BY 1/3 REV. 8:12, 13

5TH TRUMPET SCORPION BEASTS FROM HELL RELEASED WILL TORMENT 5 MOS. WON'T BE ABLE TO KILL THEM REV. 9:1-11

7TH TRUMPET RELEASE OF 7 LAST PLAGUES. RELEASED IN RAPID SUCCESSION OR SIMULTANEOUSLY REV. 15:5-16:1

1ST TRUMPET ALL GRASS BURNT. 1/3 OF TREES ALSO BURNT UP. REV. 8:7

2ND TRUMPET METEOR FALLS TO EARTH 1/3 OF SHIPS, FISH & OCEAN DESTROYED REV. 8:8, 9

YEAR 4

YEAR 5

YEAR 6

2ND HALF OF TRIBULATION PERIOD BEGINS

ANTICHRIST GOES INTO TEMPLE DECLARES HIMSELF TO BE GOD; ANTICHRIST IS ASSASSINATED THEN LATER RISES AGAIN REV. 13:2-4

DESCRIPTION OF MYSTERY BABYLON: RICHES COUNTRY IN WORLD. MADE WORLD RICH. VERY POWERFUL MILITARILY COULD BE U.S.A. REV. 17 & 18

FOLLOWING RESURRECTION SATAN ATTACKS JEWS; JEWS SCATTERED. FLEE TO PETRA REV. 12:13-17

FALSE PROPHET ERECTS STATUE; STATUE TALKS COMMANDS WORSHIP OF ANTICHRIST & TO TAKE HIS MARK 666. ALL WHO REFUSE MUST BE KILLED REV. 13:11-17

7TH BOWL HAILSTONES FALL TO EARTH 100 LBS WORLDWIDE EARTHQUAKE ISLAND'S DISAPPEAR REVELATION 16:17-21

Calvaryprophecy.com

Other Survival Resources

Making Primitive Stone Tools: Articles & Videos
http://www.wildernesscollege.com/primitive-stone-tools.html

Mountainsurvival.com: Mountain Training & Tips
http://mountainsurvival.com/

Beginning Farmer: Techniques &Instruction
https://attra.ncat.org/attra-pub/local_food/startup.html

Wild Food Survival Guide: How To Identify Wilderness Food
https://ofthefield.com/resources/products_detail.php?ProductID=4

Food Shelf Life Chart, Food That Last Forever, Storage, Etc.
http://urbansurvivalsite.com/

REI Survival: Gear
http://www.rei.com/

The Survival Zone: Backpacks, Tents, Gas Masks, Etc.
http://www.thesurvivalzone.com/

Survival Topics: Road Kill, Bark, Foraging & Other Topics
http://www.survivaltopics.com/

Survival Vegetable Gardening: Tips & Techniques

http://www.vegetable-gardening-with-lorraine.com/survival-gardening.html

How To Choose A Water Purifier
http://www.smart-camping-guide.com/camping-water-filter.html

Primitive Survival: Hunting, Trapping, Fishing, Snares, Etc.
http://www.wildwoodsurvival.com/index.html

Tips For Using Everyday Items For Other Uses
http://www.tipking.co.uk/Use_stuff/Unusual_uses/

www.ingramcontent.com/pod-product-compliance
Lightning Source LLC
Chambersburg PA
CBHW032002040426
42448CB00006B/460